THE OTHER
WOMAN

a memoir

AMINA PANKEY

Printed in the United States of America
First Printing, 2017
ISBN 978-0-9985210-0-8

13th & Joan
500 N. Michigan Avenue, Suite #500
Chicago, IL 60611

WWW.13THANDJOAN.COM

TABLE OF CONTENTS

For Cori and Bronx. One day you will read this and understand how important you are to me. You will never know how much you kept me sane. You saved my life.

To all the women that had to endure the pain of love caused by a man.

CHAPTER 1:
No Place Like Home

I LOVE MY PARENTS. I wouldn't trade them for the world. They are the most amazing people on this planet in my eyes.

My mom, who is a lot like me, is a very sweet soul. Not a mean strand exists in her being. She is literally the nicest person I know, which is why she has been run over a lot in her life. Even though that is the case, she would never change and I love that about her. She would never let the world make her hard or tough. My mother is who she is and has always been. Growing up I cannot even remember her yelling at me or any of my sisters.

On top of that, she is absolutely gorgeous, even now at sixty years old, but especially in her twenties when she had us. Mom is fully German and looks the part: blonde hair (now grey), grey/green eyes (identical to my daughter Cori's), and a slim figure with curves in all the right places! I am not surprised that my dad wasn't able to leave her side back in the 80s.

Even as an extremely free spirit, she taught us how to be independent and responsible. She never had a driver's license or a cellphone in her entire life and never wanted or needed either. She's never owned a computer or laptop. As a matter of fact, she is scared of anything electrical. She is very health oriented and has always been an artsy person. She makes jewelry by hand and draws insanely well, but she has never been able to make her art a business, unfortunately, because she deserves reward for her amazing work. I remember when we were little our transportation method was always a bicycle, kids seats attached, one in front and one on the back for my twin sister Jazz and I (our older sis Sophie was old enough to ride her own).

Mom taught us that beauty does not lie in the eye and that it's about much more than looks, and she taught us that happiness does not come from being rich in things but rich with love. She showed me and my sisters what real love means. I remember how much I loved being at home as a child, unlike other children who always loved being at our house more than their own home. The energy in our home was just so peaceful and kids were allowed to be kids. We were allowed to do a lot of things others weren't: get dirty, eat on the couch, be loud, be naked . . . just be wild and free! As long as it was peaceful, there were no rules at home—none! And even though some may think that is not a good way of raising kids, I think it was amazing and I will always cherish my childhood!

Our dad was a little more strict and rough around the edges; I think it's the African in him. As you can imagine, being that he is African, he looks the part as well: Black, nicely built (before he gained a bunch of weight with age), and extremely handsome, definitely back in the day (he even used to model a bit). The women definitely were after him, and although Mom told us she had dated quite a few black men back before she had us, for some reason she got stuck with our dad and made him the one! It could have been many things, but one thing I definitely know about my dad is that he is super-duper intelligent. I know my mom is drawn to a wise being (I must have inherited that from her also), and my dad was, and is, just that. Him being the tough one, he taught us how to deal with the world outside our home and made us understand that this is a cruel world in which people can be vicious and mean. He, like my mom, was a joy to be around. Although he was slightly harsh at times and his way of raising us differed from our Mom's, that made us respect him and we knew it was out of love.

All my memories from childhood with him include music—him playing the guitar, playing the saxophone, and having a huge collection of LPs in the house. He also had a small electronic drum machine that he still owns to this day. I used to love playing with it. Almost every night after bath time, we would dance while our dad played DJ and put on his favorite tunes. It used to be our favorite part of the day. We ran around in circles naked in the living room and came up with different moves while Mom sat in her favorite rocking chair just laughing and smiling at her three angels. Dad would make up dancing and singing games and we just were in a zone. Other times, he let us choose what LP we wanted to listen to. I remember always picking the yellow one with the Spanish music. I was maybe three or four years old, and I only knew the music each LP had by its cover.

Throughout the day, we would listen to a lot of Jazz music. Some of my parents' favorites were Miles Davis, Charlie Parker, and John Coltrane. We were exposed to some of the greats early on and it would bring a vibe to our home that was super special. When Dad was at work and Mom had a little time in between juggling all our needs, she would always use that time to listen to loud music through her headphones sitting on her rocking chair or dancing. I loved that she loved it so much, and I would sometimes sit on her lap trying to feel how she felt because I could tell it was a great feeling, and when mom was happy, we were happy!

My parents never got married, but neither did a lot of other couples we knew and that were friends of our family. Marriage in general was just not as big as I later learned it is in America. We never spoke about it, it wasn't a big deal, and we were a family anyway. My mom never really believed in it, and that was that. I think it made me see that it's not necessary to be married to have love, and it also let me know that other things matter more. Anyway, it felt like they were married, and every one of our friends from school assumed they were.

Dad would yell at us for little things like if one of us lost the remote control or if something wasn't clean, or if his food wasn't ready after work, he would be grumpy towards mom. He also would brush our little afro hair and did not care if it hurt. We had to be quiet and take it.

Mom would never do that! She would just not brush our hair at all if we didn't want it and just let us leave the house any kind of way. If we didn't wanna take a bath, we didn't take a bath. If we wanted to be up late, we were up late. She would let us pick what we want to wear. She would literally let us do whatever we wanted. She was so nice that she never yelled at her own daughters, even when Sophie became a teenager and would yell at Mom and intimidate her. Crazy, now that I think about it.

We did not have much. Matter of fact, we were poor. My mom was taking care of us while my dad worked all day and sometimes night. My sisters and I never had fancy things or expensive toys. We didn't live in a big house like some of our friends and classmates. We never went on vacation. There was just no money for that. But we were fine. We had love.

It also made us become very creative. When we started going to school, we learned how to do our own hair, braids, and such. We didn't have enough money to go to the "afro shop" (there were only two in Hamburg at the time) to get our head braided, so we learned how to do it ourselves. Same with clothing—we didn't have money to buy nice clothes, so we started buying fabric, which was way cheaper, and designed our own outfits. I don't know why, but we had these signature coats that all our friends wanted, made out of animal print fabric. In truth, we just used whatever kind we could find. To this day, we still joke about the "Kuh Mantel" (Cow Coat), which was made with a thin, black-and-white cow-print fabric. They weren't coats you would wear when it was cold, but they were perfect to throw over anything on a summer night, paired with some platform heels—that was the style back then, and we loved it because no one had them but us.

From doing our own nails to learning how to put on makeup at an early age, the three of us did it all! Going out to eat was something that happened, like, never! Thus, we learned how to cook from our mom. We didn't take dance classes, join swimming groups, or all those other things kids would do. We just couldn't afford that, but we loved being creative, so we started our own dancing group.

My twin Jazz became obsessed with choreography. Janet Jackson was her idol. We used to study her videos for hours, pressing pause every other second and rewinding to learn all of her dance moves. We were so determined to be like our favorite stars in any and every way. It was what we did for fun, and it made us proud every time we mastered something new.

But I did have some issues accepting myself throughout puberty. I hated how I looked. I didn't like the fact that I was so shy. I wanted to be skinny and have straight hair and a different shape. Confidence was something I didn't have. At fourteen, I fell into a year of heavy depression. I felt ugly and I felt like nobody liked me, when in reality I just didn't like me. I felt different and misunderstood. I ate my insecurities up inside, and in that phase, I cried every night. I was just wishing to be someone else. I literally hated everything about me from my name to my hair to the way I talked or, rather, the way I didn't talk much.

I did not share this with my mom or my sisters, but I think they realized something was wrong with me when I developed an eating disorder. I was a chubby teenager, at least compared to all the other kids in school and growing up in Germany, a world where being skinny was the only way to be "beautiful." I always felt like I was not enough. This feeling lasted a couple of years, and I wrote about it in a journal because I just did not think that anyone would understand how I felt. I got skinny as a stick, and at the same time, sick to the point that if I ate a whole apple a day instead of half an apple I felt guilty. Between me and my twin Jazz, she was always the slimmer one that everyone complimented on her look. When I had lost every inch of fat, however, I definitely was the winner in being "skinny." But only for a little while. It had to end. And though I finally felt good looking in the mirror, I still felt horrible inside.

How did it stop? I just said to myself: enough. I was unhealthy and I knew it. I took back control over my body and my life. There was not one thing that woke me up; I just grew up and grew out of that "moment" I'd had.

Have gone through that, part of me was definitely feeling different.

Being a black kid in Germany was not easy. Even though it seemed there were more and more of us "mixed kids," I was always reminded of the fact that even though I felt German, spoke German, and was around all Germans, I was not like them. I was black. We were black.

Our mom told us when we were really young that people would not believe we were her children and would ask her how long she'd had us and if we "climb on trees" like monkeys. So much for "racist Germany."

I have never been to Africa and never learned about the culture as much as I should have, but I remember being super interested in it and hearing stories from my dad about the life there and about all our relatives that we have never met. We used to take pictures for my dad to send to Senegal and we still do. To this day, I have never traveled there, but it's on my bucket list!

When our parents separated, it was hard for all of us, but I knew and understood at eight years old that it needed to happen. I didn't know why, but I trusted my mom that her decision to not want to be with dad anymore was the right one. The process of him moving out seemed to take forever. I was scared a lot because I remember feeling like I didn't really know him as he had lost a lot of weight and changed his attitude, not towards us, but towards mom. It was tough. My dad put my mom through a lot, but he eventually showed us that sticking together is what family is about when he came back into our lives a few years later. And no matter the circumstances, we all (including our mom) are what matters and family comes before anything. His mentality is just that. All we got is us! And although he is someone who likes to criticize anything and everything, he's always given his last dime and with no doubt would give his last drop of blood for any of us.

I think my dad would have loved it if one of us or all of us would have gone to college and become something other than an artist, but at the same time, our happiness is what he always supported.

I hated school so much! I hated anything where I had to be social with others. I was a kid that wanted to do everything right. Basically, I was always thinking about others and how they see me, how I might look to them, and what teachers might think of me. Never looking at myself, I lived to please others. I had no ego. When we did assignments in groups, I was always last to find a group. I let others pick their seats on school bus trips and would take the last open one. A lot of times, I would end up at a boys table when there were new seating arrangements or group activities because I never showed or said what I wanted or I just got overheard. Yeah, that was me. I wasn't happy being this way, but it was the only way I knew how to be. I didn't make friends unless I was approached. I was too shy. But I wished I could be more popular. Whenever a girl liked me and asked me to hang out, I was happy, but I remember when the age came where girls in my class started to have "boyfriends." I was just terrified of the idea. When a boy asked me if I wanted to be his "girlfriend," I would just run away.

My twin sister and I never wanted to be in the same class, because we wanted people to see us as individuals as opposed to "one." All our lives, it had been "the twins" when spoken of us, and I felt like I wanted to be my own person. So in our school years, we always chose to be separated. Having a twin was nothing special to me being that I was one and it was just normal. At times, I honestly wished we were just sisters. That (and everything else!) completely changed as I grew older. And today, I'm super grateful to know what this kind of bond feels like!

In 1994, our family grew as my mom gave birth to our youngest sister May with her new boyfriend. We were so excited, and I will always think back on that time as one of the most beautiful times in my life. I think helping to raise her shaped me to become the mother I am today. From the day May was born, I remember not wanting to do anything but to hold her. I was only eleven, but I would sit in the rocking chair for hours and hours while she slept on my chest. I would smell her and just feel so much love for her. I would go to school in the morning anticipating my return, and I would rush home like a crazy person just to be able to be with my baby sister. Thinking back on how it felt, I can compare it today to how I feel about my own babies. There is no greater love.

I never got into trouble or anything that I would get punished for. I was a picture perfect "innocent" child. So my sisters never had to stand up for me, but if anything, it would have been Sophie, our older sis, who spoke up for the three of us when there was a need. Especially when we started singing together. Time and time again, we would get into arguments with people we worked with, and the person to sort it all out was always Sophie. She was not scared to speak her mind to an adult. I honestly admired that. She was the voice for the three of us, and without her, we would have been lost for sure.

All in all, what I feel shaped me the most from my childhood is the freedom we had as kids. Becoming a teenager and then an adult, it was often taken from me and I always realize that it is what I need to be happy. So it's been a constant fight to retain something that's so important in my life. Freedom!

I also feel that because of what I went through as a teenager, hating myself and being so insecure, and then finally learning to accept me and starting to love who I am in my twenties, the years it took and the battles I fought within myself, the contrast from then to now is so much more extreme. Now, I am just so proud of who I am, and it's amazing that, although it took years and years, it was possible for me to become the woman that I am today.

"I'll Be the One There"

BY AMINA & JAZZ BUDDAFLY

Free as the wind, I wanna be free like an angel,
I was so lost within, couldn't be myself and that caused failure.
Something inside came and said to me where is your life?
Realization was the key cause now I'm fine. . . .

"You Won't Be Stopping Me"
BY ME (LATER ON)

Call me different,
Say I don't fit in,
My ways, my looks, my style,
You might not like it
But I won't fight it.
Just keep staring.
I don't give a damn,
Because I am myself,
So hate it or love it,
But you won't be stopping me.

CHAPTER 2:
Do You Believe in Magic?

D O YOU BELIEVE IN MAGIC? I did. There are times when you just know. We knew that we had something special, and we wanted the world to hear not only our voices but also what we had to say. We made magic together. Our voices together sounded like "butter"—that's what the amazing and legendary record mogul himself Mr. L.A. Reid told us years later when we auditioned for him at the Def Jam offices in New York. And that is also how we were later named "Black Butterfly." But now, in this moment, meeting someone like him was only a dream that seemed so far away. . . .

I remember from my childhood that music was always a big part of our everyday life. My dad would play music at home all day long. He was a fan of classical music, as well as salsa and jazz. It was normal for me and my sisters to sing and dance around the house all the time. Our dad loved making up songs while talking to us, and one of my favorite things used to be dancing to "Peter und der Wolf," a children's story told by symphonies in an orchestra. I didn't know it then, but I learned so much about music from those moments. From being exposed to different genres and just from singing along, not with vocals, but with instruments.

I remember me and my sisters never wanting to sing in unison but always sing our own note, which is how we became so good at singing in harmony. It was a completely natural thing for us.

When we joined kid's choir at the age of six, we became even more passionate. We were not the outgoing type of kids; we were the quiet ones, the underdogs, at least me and Jazz. Sophie was two years older and was a little more "experienced" and vocal. But the three of us always felt like we could teach the other kids something. There were a lot of kids who sang louder, were more outgoing, more confident, and less shy, but when it came to the musicality, Sophie, Jazz and I just knew that we had something they all didn't. We never acted that way though. We tried to blend in and just be part of the group, but it did shine through. When it came down to it and we had to learn a new song or melody or harmony, the choir teacher looked at us to demonstrate. It didn't make me feel special, just different.

But during this time, singing wasn't just something we did in our free time anymore. It had become our life.

As we grew into our teenage years, we discovered R&B music, and singing in a choir wasn't cool enough anymore. I guess when you're that age you look for something to identify with, and for me, in the early 90s that definitely was Mariah Carey. I became a diehard fan who studied all of her music, songs, riffs, adlibs, and backgrounds. I would sing her songs, not understanding a lot of what she was saying. I would dream of being on a stage singing like her. When I listened to Mariah, I just was in a happy space, even the sad songs. But there was just so many new groups and singers we had fallen in love with, every week we would go to the record store and find a new "imported" R&B album by some group or singer from America no one in Germany had ever heard of. It felt great discovering all this music and not listening to what everyone else was listening to but having something that only us three knew about. Girl groups like S.H.E., Before Dark, Brownstone, En Vogue, Jade, Blaque, Allure, For Real, and of course TLC and Destiny's Child (the list goes on and on). So many black girls making music, and amazing music at that, doing what we wanted to do. Making music that had swag, soul, harmonies, and was of good quality.

We just felt we were like them, but what we didn't have was the music, the songs. We had the look and the voices, but we weren't able to make music like them, because we were in Germany where music like that just was not made.

I would read the booklets and study all of the producers' names and styles . . . to the point that I would know who produced a song as soon as I listened to it without reading booklets. I really believe the 90s were the reason and the motivation for us to take this group thing seriously.

All this great music came from America, but we were only in Germany. Little old Germany, which didn't have music we loved. None! We hated the music at home. The charts were filled with dumbed-down dance tracks. No musicality or soul, just stupid lyrics and techno beats. Or songs in German, which I never could see us doing. Singing in German just didn't sound right to me. Popular music in Germany was literally disgusting to me at the time. We felt like we did not belong there, because we liked "real" music and there was none! We wanted to sing in harmony, and no one wanted to hear that in Germany. It wasn't something people understood.

When we got signed by BMG logic in Germany at the ages of fourteen and sixteen, it was bittersweet. At first, I was excited, so much so that I left school at fifteen to concentrate on the group. This was something our teachers had recommended because I specifically hated school, and when I was not interested in something, I was just not able to learn it. My mind would shut down, so I fell off and the teachers noticed. I knew what I wanted to do with my life at this point. I was smart and good at school but excelled only at what I was interested in. I had always loved things like astronomy, geography, art, and languages, so I had good grades, but when it came to math, chemistry, and sports, I sucked because I simply had no interest. I also was not very social and hated being at school, interacting with people or kids. I didn't have many friends, but everyone liked me; I was just quiet and not one to draw attention to herself.

So, both of my sisters and I took a break from school for now, thinking we would be stars instead, but, really, it was the beginning of feeling pressured and imprisoned by the music business. Being told how to be an artist when you are already one is just something I couldn't deal with even at just fifteen years old. No, we didn't know much about the business, but we knew about music from the life we had lived—from the studying we had done on our own, from our dad schooling us unintentionally, and just by listening. You learn so much from listening. And we felt like we had listened way more in our lifetime than these German people without rhythm who were now telling us how to sing, when they couldn't even hold a note. Anyway, that just brought my sisters and me closer together because we understood each other, and they didn't understand us! It was frustrating.

We knew at this time that Germany wasn't the place for us, but America was just too far and too big and too unreachable.

A few years later, however, we had saved up to buy plane tickets. The destination: JFK. New York City was calling.

We didn't know what to expect; we just were super excited to get to New York for the very first time. It seemed so far away. But we were on our way.

We had only saved up enough money for a week, so we were going to "test the waters" and come back. But this trip turned out to be life changing.

We were motivated by American artists we had met at concerts in Germany (like Missy Elliot, Busta Rhymes, DJ Scratch, or road managers and other musicians I can't remember) who told us that we should come to America. Whenever an artist we liked had a concert in Hamburg, we would go and wait backstage, hoping to meet someone who could help us get connected overseas.

We had always gotten such great response from Americans. Whenever we sang acapella, people were blown away. And that just continued to happen once we landed in New York.

We were completely unprepared. We didn't even know where we were going to stay when we landed at JFK. Of course, we had not told our parents that, but we literally were lost once we got there. I was just glad that we had Sophie—our oldest, the protector, the speaker, the one that was not shy. Sophie was twenty-one at the time. Jazz and I were nineteen and very intimidated by everything. The only thing we knew how to do was sing. But even talking was not something we were comfortable doing, because we felt that our English was just not good enough.

Our parents, especially our mom, had always been very lenient. They separated when I was eight, our dad left, and we didn't see him for a few years. My parents were never married so there was no divorce; our dad just had to leave because of the issues he and my mom had. It was a very bad and long process and a very difficult one for all parties involved. But, eventually, it was just us and our mom who never told us what to do and always let us decide and do whatever the hell we wanted. I like to say that she is lucky my sisters and I always were good girls and never got in trouble or did stupid shit like other teenagers. However, by this time (2002), our dad was back in our lives, but he was not involved in things too much. So when it came to going to New York, he knew, but I think the thing that made both of our parents comfortable was knowing that we were together. They weren't worried about us, because they were confident we are grown and we are smart and wouldn't get caught up in anything crazy.

I will never forget the date: June 4, 2002. So here we were in the Big Apple not knowing where to start. Should we just walk up to a record label and try to meet someone? We realized even if we wanted to, that kind of thing was not possible here, because every building has security and you have to have a meeting scheduled to even get inside. Like I said, we were just lost upon arrival and definitely overwhelmed. But we had made it here! So we were not going to quit trying now. We ended up walking the streets of New York, taking in the energy, and that alone made us feel powerful. We were here! People were looking at us; we had a style that you just had to look at and that just stood out. We would get stopped constantly on the street and we'd sing wherever, whenever! We were always ready. I remember it like yesterday. I never experienced heat like this—90 degrees and humidity! It was insane. We had checked into the Roosevelt Hotel on 45th Street and Madison, but we had only enough money for three nights. What had we gotten ourselves into?

Anyway, we took it day by day. Sophie called the one number we had from a DJ we had met in Germany, Busta Rhymes' DJ Scratch. He had loved meeting us in Germany and thought we were super talented, so he gave us his info, and now he said welcome to New York. Unfortunately, they were still on the road, so we couldn't connect. We were just hoping to get introduced to someone. Anyone. Luckily, we met a lot of people in the first few days who helped us find our way around and check out the right places just by walking through Manhattan. We even managed to perform at a place called Joe's Pub on day four I believe.

Our big sis Sophie had run into a guy in the hotel lobby who named himself Prince, who was someone who got around and knew a lot of people. He was the type of dude you would never ever see in Germany. We had only seen guys like him in movies so this was very surreal. He was wearing a hat, had gold teeth and a cane, and wore a white suit. Sophie brought him up to our hotel room to meet us, and as soon as he saw us and heard us sing, he picked up the phone and started calling people to tell them he had just ran into the most beautiful, talented girls ever. "They look like Beyoncé but ten times prettier. . . . They sing like the Supremes," I remember him saying over and over. We were excited. He took us to Battery Studios on our first night. I remembered how many of my favorite artists had recorded here, and I was in awe. He also took us to a club somewhere downtown in Manhattan. Mind you, Jazz and I were only nineteen, but we got in without a problem. We hung out next to P. Diddy and Kelis all night and just thought this was all a dream. But it wasn't. This was only the beginning of a very, very long and intense journey.

Performing at Joe's Pub gave us some "shine," and we got approached by multiple people in the business, including a music manager and a couple of entertainment lawyers who, over the next year or so, helped us out here and there, even if it was just giving us a place to stay as we continued to travel back and forth from Germany to NYC. We were determined to make it in America! We knew we had what it would take! We finally felt challenged, but that was a good thing! Everyone was so talented here unlike at home, where it really felt like there wasn't any competition. We loved being recognized in the way we got recognized. It was completely a new world. So much bigger and better, it just felt right, like this was where we needed to be! I don't know how it happened, but even though Sophie was the leader of the group, I was the lead singer, always singing verses and main parts in a song and always standing in the middle when we would sing together. That became even more pronounced once we started recording. I can't remember how many times we made the trip, but we did a lot of traveling back and forth from Germany to NYC over the next two years. Not only would we continuously run out of money, but we also weren't allowed to stay in the states longer than 90 days at a time as German tourists.

So we would always go back home to work and to go on tour with a gospel group for a couple of months to save up more money . . . for more traveling.

Every time we came back to NYC, we would stay with someone that we had met the last time or someone that we had gotten cool with. We had stayed in every borough from Brooklyn to Harlem to Manhattan to Queens and even Jersey City. Lots of times we slept on the floor for months without blankets or anything. But we didn't care; we had never known luxury, and we were just happy to be there. We didn't need anything but each other. We would ride the subway to go to clubs in hopes of meeting more people who could help us. One time, we had gotten into an argument with the guy we were staying with and he kicked us out. We were literally on the street with all our bags and belongings without a penny in pocket or any idea where to go and no money to go back to the airport. These kind of situations happened many times. But the three of us were fearless. We tried out working with different managers, different up-and-coming producers who offered us to record for free. We did a lot!

In 2004, we had been auditioning for a lot of record label A&Rs and even VPs at times through this young dude O that we had made our first official manager. Every meeting we took seemed promising, and people seemed intrigued by our uniqueness! However, in the end, it just seemed like all these labels had either just signed a group or had a big girl group in their roaster. We kept trying nonetheless. . . .

"Black Buddafly"
(A SONG I WROTE ABOUT LEAVING GERMANY)

Looking out my window thinking I wish I could fly,
Be free like a bird, fluttering like a butterfly,
Out into the world full of excitement and energy,
And may no storm, no rain, nothing stop me.
I feel like I just wanna break out of nowhere,
Into another world and I hope I won't be scared,
I'm looking for a place to fill my soul. I'm flying away. . . .

Black butterfly fly away, towards the sun,
Make your way, up to the sky, into your destiny.
Black buddafly don't forget, you've gotta come,
Come back, never forget where you're from,
It's just not where you belong.

CHAPTER 3:
Sound Check

BEING IN NEW YORK and experiencing a whole new world was amazingly exciting. When my sisters and I first decided to go to NYC, we thought of it more like a trip and we didn't plan on actually "moving," but we just fell in love with the way people loved us in America, and it made us love ourselves more and become more confident. Especially me. I didn't feel so "different" anymore. Because everyone was "different" here. Also, there were a lot more brown skin girls and black people in general. I started feeling good about myself—very good!

New York is a place where you have all types of people. People from all over the world. It's so multicultural, and we were not used to that, but we loved everything about it . . . except how expensive it was and how quickly we would run out of money.

Going back and forth for a couple of years became a routine. We were always pulled back to the states, and whenever we had to go back to Germany, we couldn't wait to get back to NYC. With each trip, we made something new happen, met more people, and recorded more songs. It felt like we were doing something with our life, something major that we couldn't feel in Germany, something that could become very special. As there really hadn't been anyone of German origin who had "made it in America," we felt we could become the exception.

People in Germany, including ex managers and producers, thought we were crazy wanting to take on such a hard road. However, they were not in our shoes, and they didn't know what happened every time we went to NYC. They didn't know how much more we felt accepted and understood as artists.

I never missed Germany. I missed my parents a little bit, but there was just too much happening, and I felt like we had tunnel vision. We were just so very determined and wanted to do this so bad that missing home, even if we did, had to wait. . . .

The way we got approached by men was so different in New York. Actually, I never knew how it felt, and I think all three of us were flattered (at first) because it would happen all the time in New York but NEVER at home. Until it started getting annoying, which took a few years, we liked the attention and the fact that we didn't have to be skinny or white to be desired by men. Up until this point in my life, I had only had two real boyfriends, and both of these relationships, if I can call them that, weren't really long term. I loved imagining, thinking, and writing about this thing called love, but the reality was that I was way too focused on where I wanted to go in my life to be distracted by men.

At one point, we lived in East Harlem on 1st Avenue and East 118th Street in a two-bedroom apartment that belonged to a production trio of three guys that took us in. Sophie, Jazz, and I shared a tiny room upstairs. We slept on top of our clothes because there was no bed, mattress, or blankets. But we were happy to have a place to stay, and we were used to this kind of "housing" while in New York. And at this particular time, we were even happier that they had a recording studio in the house that we were able to use every day. I learned and wrote a lot during these three months.

I started seeing that musically I was the one who contributed the most to the group. Creative juices were flowing, and most of it came from me. We were making demo after demo and finally had music to shop around to labels. Without Sophie, we wouldn't have even been here; she was literally being group member and manager at the same time. And Jazz . . . well Jazz had it all going on—her style always stood out, and she swagged us out! And even though she's always super laid back and quiet, she would come up with the dopest arrangements and harmonies. She gave us flavor.

I loved the fact that I had them both. I needed them both, and I was confident in our potential. Together, the three of us were complete, and without any one of us, we would have not been as amazing as everyone thought we were. The early years in NYC were definitely the hardest, and it brought me and my sisters closer together than ever, because no one knew what it felt like. What we went through together connected us. It was a rollercoaster ride.

In 2004, we ended up spending some time in Philly because we had met some managers out there who wanted to help us. We never thought about going there, but when we had a falling out with the guy we were staying with in NYC at this particular time, and landed on the street, we had nowhere to go, and these guys from Philly were our only fallback. It was a struggle—we were broke! We didn't want to ask people for money so some days we would literally starve. . . .

But they had some connections, and somehow we were introduced to someone at the Larry Gold studio in Philly. This guy knew another guy who knew someone else that owned a production company, and it was just like the dots were connecting.

We got offered a "production deal," and a few months later, we agreed to sign.

Negotiation started and months went by where we just waited for the contract to be drafted. I was in a relationship at this time with the love of my life (as I thought); however, this man wasn't with me. We were dating long distance for a while as he traveled a lot and relocated all the time being a professional athlete. So during this waiting period, my sisters went back home, while I went to see my man wherever he was at the time. I loved him. I loved him so much, but I loved the idea of making it big with my sisters more. I was twenty-two at this time . . . so young, so hungry, so motivated and inspired. Just ready to go and do whatever it took!

Months and months of work were ahead of us, and my sisters and I eventually got put into an apartment in Baltimore, Maryland, for almost a year to work on our official album. We hated living there. The apartment was somewhere out of the city totally excluded from everything, and we were stuck in the house or in the studio most days . . . but I guess we just tried to stick to the plan of completing this project and then preparing for the big meetings they had set up for us back in NYC. It took months and months. We tried to not complain and look at this as an opportunity that many would be dying to have.

And when the day came in 2005, the drive back to New York was the most nerve wracking ever because we knew we were being put in front of some major people.

First stop, Russell Simmons' office. He had just started his new music group, RSMG, and he made us the first act to be signed. There was no question. . . . He loved us right away—the fact that we were foreign, our look, our sound, everything about us was polished at this point. We had been working out, and we looked great! We met everyone at his office, and his then-wife Kimora Lee was also involved in our image/fashion.

His distribution was through Island Def Jam, so we had to audition for the CEO, Mr. L.A. Reid. I was *so* nervous. I knew this was the man that signed and "made" TLC, Toni Braxton, Usher, Pink (who was a fairly new artist we loved back then), Avril Lavigne, and the list goes on. I was especially nervous because I felt like I was the one to make or break this opportunity as I was singing lead. We sang acapella, opening with "Yesterday" by the Beatles (but En Vogue's version) and, after that, a song I had written called "When I'm with You."

I felt like I blew it because of my nerves, but L.A. just looked at us the entire time and didn't interrupt. After we finished, he said, "Y'all sound like butter, but can you sing that last song one more time . . . but really sing it this time?" I didn't know how to feel about that, but I guess I was glad to get a chance to make it right, and I definitely sang it better the second time.

Then, it was a wrap.

He did not say anything else to us after, but we left his office and knew we had a record deal. It felt amazing. Unreal, but great. We felt accomplished. This was our first big success in America. Even though it took a while for negotiations, we eventually signed an album deal and the *real* journey began. . . .

Although we had just spent almost a year working super hard on music and everything else that artist development requires, we were once again put to work, tasked with more recording. But everything felt "official" now. We had a budget and were put with stylists, choreographers, songwriters, etc. They picked a single, we shot our first video, and photoshoots were happening left and right. . . . The whole 9. They gave our album a release date and sent us on the road to start promoting the song "Rock-A-Bye," our first single (2005).

These were fun times. . . . Def Jam had a bunch of new artists. We didn't know who any of them were, but we were introduced to them and started doing a bunch of shows together. One was R&B singer and songwriter Ne-Yo, and then there was this Caribbean girl everyone talked about named Rihanna. Also joining us on the promo tour was another new artist, this kid from Virginia named Chris Brown. He blew me away every single time we watched him do his thing! He was just so damn talented—at only sixteen years old.

For me, it was hard being that I had gotten engaged in the middle of all this but wasn't able to see my fiancé more than once every three months for a few days at a time. I hated it. I cried a lot. But we were so busy that I wasn't able to do anything about it or stay sad for a long period of time; I just got used to the situation. I had chosen to do this, so now I had to deal with it.

My sisters and I really thought we were going to blow up with this album, especially since people loved us and our song wherever we went. The song was playing on the radio everywhere, and we had to visit countless radio stations, do interviews, and attend events with Russell Simmons. We were constantly traveling and performing.

We always stayed the same, but people looked at us in a different light. We were a signed group with a song on the radio, and to a lot of people, that meant we were of more value, but the way we grew up, we knew we were exactly the same girls we had always been. We found it a bit annoying that all of a sudden people cared and thought we mattered, but we learned quickly that this is just how it is. . . . We learned to appreciate the fact that there was a demand for Black Buddafly. We felt we were on the right path.

However, when it came to picking the second single, we started having some mixed feelings and issues with our record label. I was happy because Jazz and I had written the second single, but I was not happy with the way it sounded. I didn't like how they had mixed and arranged my vocals on the song I wrote, and I was not happy with the video we shot.

There were a lot of things I didn't like. For one, we didn't love the direction that we were being marketed in. We knew what kind of group we were, but it seemed they had their own agenda. Our production team and Russell Simmons chose another "urban" song called "Bad Girl," but we had heard that our actual label Def Jam and the man in charge, L.A. Reid, wanted to put out one of our more pop-oriented records. There were a lot of people in the mix, and a lot of confusion and uncertainty started to happen on everyone's end. One day, we were up at the Def Jam office, and they told us that "Jay" wanted to see us. I was confused—who is Jay? On the way to the elevator, I realized they were talking about Jay Z, CEO at Roc Nation, which was also a joint-venture label under Def Jam.

I didn't know what this was about, but we just went in his office, sat down, and started talking. He asked about our project, our album, and how everything was going. The fact that he was interested to hear about Black Buddafly's project felt good.

We told him we had just shot our second video, but we didn't love it. We told him we were just hoping this song would be our real hit. He then asked to see the video, and they brought the final cut, which had just arrived from the editors. Afterwards, he gave me the best advice ever. I expressed that I wasn't happy with how my vocals sounded on the song, and he said, "Why do you have them sounding like that then? Why, if you don't like the video, is it coming out?" He kept going about how we as the artists have to make sure we absolutely love what we do. I agreed, but it was hard. He mentioned Kanye West (who at this time wasn't nearly as cocky and "out there" as he is now) and how we should be a little more like him, and I agreed again, but it was difficult. Up until then, we had always heard that what we needed to do was listen to the people that had had success, so going against that when we had waited for this opportunity forever seemed wrong. We decided to try to find middle ground, still compromise and listen, but not let them make us feel like puppets. This kind of situation reminded us of when we were signed in Germany as teenagers; it was a lot to deal with, so many opinions and people that we tried to make happy, but at the end of the day, it was just impossible. Sophie started being very annoyed and exhausted because she was the one still talking for us most of the time, and it just felt like there was no way to win.

Anyhow, we released the second single, and it turned out to be a pretty good thing, putting us back on tour and creating a buzz around Black Buddafly. It even put us on the soundtrack for a movie called *Waist Deep* and a major TV show. However, it never became a huge hit, and they ended up pushing back our album's release date three times and, in the end, didn't put it out at all.

Even though it definitely wasn't all the way "us," I liked our album, and it was a bummer that no one ever got to hear it, even to this day.

This is just a typical example of how a major record deal doesn't work out, and Black Buddafly, after another few years, would go through the same situation once more. As a duo this time.

CHAPTER 4:
Will Work for Food

FTER BEING released from Def Jam in 2006, Sophie left the group to go back to Germany. She had found out that she was pregnant and was super fed up with the music industry and everything we had endured dealing with these sharks, as we liked to say.

The struggle was real. At first, Jazz and I thought that it would be impossible to continue the group without our backbone, our mom of the group, our vocal advocate, Sophie.

But we decided to stay in New York and continue to push forward with music.

We were missing a major part sound all of a sudden, and we weren't able to blow people away with our harmonies anymore. We needed something new, a plan, but also something to give us back that fire, that "specialness."

I still believed we were meant to make it big. And this was the time that, even though we were broke, I spent my last seventy dollars on a tattoo on my wrist that says "Superstar." The guy who had initially signed Black Buddafly in 2004 gave us three nicknames, and they stuck with us. Sophie was "Mother Teresa," Jazz was "Trouble," and I was "Superstar."

I loved it, simply because I felt like I was one! Despite the fact that I really wasn't yet! It motivated me to keep going. Another thing that I did was buy a cheap Casio 66 keyboard and started teaching myself to play. I fell in love with the instrument. I would sit at home and play sometimes up to six hours a day just learning songs by ear. Classical pieces like the "Waltz in D-flat major, Op. 64" by Chopin. I had no clue about chords or anything technical when it came to playing; I just played, listened, and copied. Note by note. I started coming up with original songs shortly after.

The first song I ever wrote on keys was entitled "Time," and most ironically, it spoke about heartbreak, which is something I experienced shortly after writing it. I didn't write it about me or what I was going through. The song just came to me, and I thought it was crazy that, after writing it, my breakup happened.

The song was special not only because it was the first song I composed, but also because it was almost like we had developed a new sound. Was the keyboard replacing Sophie? Sometimes I felt that way. . . .

My then fiancé' and I just couldn't come to terms with this long distance thing. We would argue way too much and decided mutually over the phone that we needed to "take a break." Which is exactly what happened. Then, the break turned into a breakup. And I didn't get to see him again until a year later. But it was the end of us. I was hurt, but I was okay. Until I read on the internet a couple of months later that he was getting married to a girl I had been suspicious about him cheating on me with. It was traumatic. But *time* is what got me through it. I enjoyed being single and alone with my newfound passion of composing for the next few years. I started recording Jazz and me at home and mixing our own songs. I really put all my energy into creating and learning.

I was in my mid-twenties, and I was working on my genius, bettering my skills every day. We were also living it up, partying whenever we had money to travel from Brooklyn to Manhattan (which is not expensive at all, but we were broke all the time). I really came into my own in those years, and I would never give that time back, even though saying that we struggled is an understatement. This time contributed in a big way to me becoming *me*.

"Time"

It may be hard to believe, but I will be better in a week,
Probably tell you how great I am a month from now,
And if it takes another year for me to not shed another tear,
I know that I'll be fine 'cause all I need to do is give it time.

At this point in my life, having been through a major breakup and great disappointment in our career, but yet continuing to be strong and move on day by day with nothing but myself, my mind, my skills, my productivity, and, of course, my twin by my side, I felt strong. I felt like I could do anything. I had gone from not liking anything about me to loving myself more and more, and I did not need confirmation or a man or anyone to agree that what I was doing was great. It felt great! I felt great! In this time, I wrote a song called "I Love Myself," which will always be one of my favorites only because of where it came from: a real place in me. I would sit at the piano and sing with my twin; it was again magical whenever we played together.

I don't know where it came from, but I think time and all these experiences had made me grow into a woman who felt powerful.

We weren't "successful" in selling records, but I was successful creating amazing music without any help. We didn't have money, but we were in our mid-twenties and on fire—from our music to how we looked—and we felt amazing about ourselves. I definitely felt like "I'm the shit" regardless of our "status." The breakup didn't change how I saw love or how I loved. I believed that I would be in love again sooner or later, and, honestly, thinking back, getting over him was easier than it seemed at first. It was easier than any breakup that came in the years to follow (ain't that always how it goes?), and I stopped crying after a couple of weeks. . . . I did just what everyone in this world tells you to do when you go through heartbreak: focus on me and keep busy. It worked.

Jazz and I were lucky because, though we had now been without Sophie, we had one of our best friends, Esther, also from Germany living with us. Even though she wasn't part of the group, she had been part of the team for a few years now, since even before Sophie had left. She had been on the road with us and was something like our personal manager who came along any and everywhere we went. Esther was someone we could rely on for all things, and though she wasn't connected enough to get us back poppin' in the industry, she was a huge help and took a lot of stress off our shoulders when it came to dealing with people. We were glad to have her. At this time, we had moved from our nice big loft in Williamsburg, Brooklyn, to a small one-and-a-half-bedroom railroad apartment in Greenpoint, Brooklyn. It was definitely a downgrade, but we just had no choice.

We also found a new management/production situation and were confident that this company would help us as they had broken out one of the biggest female artists. . . .

Black Buddafly was a duo now, but with this new, more mature, and, as we felt, very unique sound, we believed this would be our second big shot in America at winning in this game.

CHAPTER 5:
Another Sad Love Song

MEETING OUR EXPECTATIONS, after some time passed, this new company we aligned with got us another major record deal. This time with J Records, a label we had dreamed of being with. . . . Jazz and I were happy but nervous; we knew now that being signed really does not mean much, and we just hoped that this time things would be different. We worked our asses off for months and months, writing, recording, being paired with different producers and writers, trying to find that one song that everyone would go crazy about.

I was frustrated. The company only cared about the music they had set us up to create and wasn't paying attention to the music I made, alone, at home, with my piano, in my little home studio. I felt like that music, which I made from the heart, was our treasure—but how was I going to make them see and understand this vision we had? It ended up becoming an endless battle over direction, style of music, and image. AGAIN. Basically what we had been going through since the very beginning. I continued doing me and getting better by the day.

Another song I wrote during this time was entitled "Your Love is Poison," talking about the relationship between the company and us. I had a real relationship with all my songs. Every one meant something to me, and sometimes I would sit at home playing these tunes and crying because this music had become so real and heartfelt. I felt a shift in my soul as I stopped making music just to become famous and to have a hit record and started writing simply what came pouring out of my heart. I didn't think about my music being "commercial" enough or "radio friendly" enough. Anyone that heard my stuff would encourage us to put it out, but we were stuck in a deal and we weren't allowed to put out music ourselves—that was the company's job. Only, they didn't put anything out. *Again.*

I continued writing, and my catalogue grew in a massive way. Some nights, I was tempted to go out and party, but instead I would stay in and play piano till daylight, or record two songs at the same time going back and forth.

I had a routine: Sleep in, work out in the park (being active was always a must), cook (healthy foods), and then spend the rest of the day creating!

Finishing a song filled a void in me that nothing else in the world could fill.

A lot of times, Jazz would be there with me, helping and giving her input, but other times, the compositions would be all mine, and that started to happen more and more. I developed my own lane . . . and I was proud. Because I was going nonstop making songs that she wasn't always involved in, I think Jazz had a hard time with it, and yet she never said anything because, even though she probably felt a bit left out, she loved and understood my process like no other. My creativity motivated her. And she, as my twin, just wanted to let me be me. It happened very naturally. I just did what I felt I was supposed to do. There was no plan of being a solo artist; as a matter of fact, all these songs I was making were intended for *us*, Black Buddafly.

As time went on, Jazz and I naturally started doing things separately. She had fallen in love and wasn't home all the time. I was single and dating different guys—I had fun, but never got into anything deep because my music was occupying all my time. I also was aware that the guys I liked at this time were not the type of guys to build with, to *be* with, or to take that seriously. I liked things the way they were. I dated a few athletes, some of whom had girlfriends or wives that they never told me about, but of course, I would find out and it would turn me off. . . . I also dated a couple of guys who had just gotten out of relationships, and that never worked out either. But it was okay; I wasn't looking for love. I didn't need a man to love me, because I had enough love for myself.

I felt like I was becoming who I was meant to be. But there was always more. More that I learned, more that I understood, and more that made me change. These years, during which I spent a lot of time alone really getting to know myself, were crucial in my journey to who I became. Who I am today.

Since our situation with J Records turned out to be another fail, we had to make a decision: Where do we go from here? I can proudly say that I walked out of that situation with my head held high, feeling *free*. It was like we were being held hostage.

Our music—and there was a ton of material we had worked very hard on—was shelved, and I had so much in me that wanted out, so much I wanted to share, and so much more I had to say. I had been locked down, confined to only put out music that these people approved, and needed to free myself. It was the most frustrating thing ever.

But one day, we sat down for another meeting with the bosses, and they told us to just sit tight and trust the process. I was tired, I was over it, and I felt disrespected because we were constantly talked down on. What were we waiting for? I asked myself that question over and over. . . . They would tell us we were hard to deal with and we didn't listen when I felt the opposite; I felt that I was putting my own happiness to the side to please them and compromise in such a way I said I wouldn't ever again. I thought about that talk with Jay-Z years before, and I had had enough. I knew I was somebody. I knew that I was good at what I did. Even without a "hit record." I remember slamming the office doors, saying, "Fuck that" and "Have a nice life," and I meant it. As I came out of that office building on 35th Street in Manhattan, I screamed, "I'm done!" I was *free*. I was *happy*—even though I had just lost everything!

I had no idea what would happen next, no clue how to survive or how I would eat. But I knew I was not going to be imprisoned just because I needed my rent paid, not anymore!

Another phase of struggling began for us . . . and in the end, we were evicted from our Brooklyn apartment as a result of not being able to pay rent for months. Jazz moved in with her boyfriend, Esther had gone back to Germany for a while to take care of some things, and I found myself a roommate situation with five other people in an even cheaper area in Brooklyn. I also found myself a job. A real job—something I had never had—as a musician. I scoured the Internet for ways to make money and ended up at a place that I will forever cherish and be thankful for: the legendary Village Underground.

The owner invited me to the club to audition for the house band. When the night came, I was joined by Jazz and our friend and R&B singer Tank, who we had worked with for the past year on our album with J Records that never came out. He was in New York for business, and we hadn't seen him since working in the studio in L.A. months before, so we decided to meet up to catch up. I walked into the club super confident, but when I heard the level of musicianship happening on that stage, I got super nervous. I decided to sing Mariah Carey's "Vision of Love." Why I picked that song I have no idea! It was way too hard in that environment. I sucked! To be fair, I don't think I sang horribly, but I definitely felt like I just blew it. However, the owner seemed to like me and called me to come back the next day for a private meeting. It was a bit more relaxed. I sang some Jackson 5 and an original song I had just written called "Colorblind." He loved the fact that I played keys and was not just a singer, so he called his wife to check me out, and that same night I started performing with the band. A great new phase in my life began—although, when I first joined them, I again got super intimidated by all the talent around me.

I was used to fakeness—programmed drums, Auto-Tune, and producers that sometimes didn't even play instruments. I was used to a world where everything was more about marketing, looks, sex appeal, and image than actual, real music. But now I was challenged. I was around real musicians, people who were the best of the best, vocalists who matched up to the great singers I admired growing up. It was a whole new scene, but it was exactly what I needed in order to become a better musician.

The band consisted of five singers, now including me, and five musicians, some of whom played and sang at the same time. It was a new world for me, and I absolutely loved it. I loved being there. It was fun, and it didn't even feel like work.

Besides me, there was another new female singer who had toured with numerous big artists and was insanely talented. She and I became close friends. Everyone was super nice and supportive of the new girls, and one of the male musicians caught my attention not too much later, which is a story of its own, but anyway. . . .

Here I was doing something alone. Without my sisters. Sometimes, I felt like I was supposed to be doing this; other times, I felt bad because what was happening with Black Buddafly?

In the fall of 2010, Jazz found out that she was pregnant. She wasn't doing anything exciting with her life, unlike me who was now busy with my new job. Even though it went unspoken, Black Buddafly was on hold for now. We were unsigned, and, although we did put out mixtapes and lots of original live videos on YouTube, I just didn't invest the time and effort into the group anymore. I was loving playing live every night, learning, and getting better at being a performer. I was twenty-seven, and I felt that it was time to live *my* life. Be about myself. Jazz, again, must have felt left out.

But there was also something else that was stressing her—and me—out. Our visas were expiring . . . meaning we would have to go back to Germany and apply for new permits to legally work in the states. We had done successfully at least six times over the years, but since we didn't have a record label anymore, things were a little more complicated. . . .

I had my own thing going on, so I was in a better position than Jazz, but this was never a quick process, and I wasn't able to renew my visa in time before it expired. We both were forced to go back that winter. Jazz felt that the best thing for her was having the baby in Germany, but I was devastated.

I was loving life in New York again—discovering this new music scene, making new friends, and, on top of it all, unexpectedly falling head over heels in love. Jay was his name, and he was nothing like the guys I had been dealing with, maybe because I was used to dating guys my age and he was older, maybe because he was not an "industry dude," or maybe because he was just different. We had started dating shortly after I joined the band six months before. We were being very private about us because that's how he liked it. I didn't care. At least not in the beginning. But I got to know him quickly and accepted his weird ways, even in times I didn't agree. . . . I liked to call that "compromising in a relationship." I believed in that.

But now, I was back in Germany, without him, trying to figure out my life. I hated being stuck there and not being able to be around my new love. It took me ten months to return to NYC. Ten months, and it was like I had never left. I had spent some time in Germany, but most of 2011 in Ibiza, Spain, singing at a club, which was another life-changing experience that came about by chance. I spent tons of time alone, reading, working out, writing, doing yoga, and just enjoying nature and my own company. Being a lead singer six nights a week took its toll, and I experienced a phase where I lost my voice and thought that my career was over—no, screw that—it felt like my life was over. I never knew how important my voice was until I didn't have it. I had to see doctors and perform, singing full sets with twenty percent of my instrument. I remember how much it hurt. Physically and emotionally. I got lonely at times, but Jay came to visit whenever he could. When he'd leave, I would literally count the days till I would see him again. I loved him. Of course, I had to write about it, and a song entitled "Our Song (All Yours)" came to life.

When I finally came back home to New York, though, things were different between us. It started with him not offering to let me to move in with him, my first disappointment. But I shook it off and moved in with my best friend Nycole, who lived in midtown Manhattan at the time. Still, I spent most nights at Jay's, but we started having a lot of problems because—and here we are again—there was another woman in the picture. I found out about her upon my return from Europe. What a surprise. I mean, we had spent ten months in a long-distance relationship, and I should have known that I wasn't the only one anymore. The other woman was apparently his ex, who came back in the picture while I was overseas. Or she never left, which is probably more likely.

Either way, after waiting for ten months to be back with him, I was extremely heartbroken. And this, I believe, is when I learned and understood that this is just what men do. I was convinced this is what they *all* do. They lie. They make you feel as if you're what they want. Well, they might be serious about wanting you, but you're just not the only. You're never the only. The way that I love, I didn't understand how this was possible, but I am also not a man, and I just came to terms with that being the explanation. We stayed together for a few more months, but it was nothing but drama, making up again, and then more drama. It drained me. I went back to making music and wrote a song called "Why." In this song, I asked myself why I loved him, which is a question I couldn't answer. That was my answer. . . .

It's like I'm in love with summer, but you give me spring.

Fighting through light and thunder, I'm under your wing.

We fly, and sometimes I wonder, am I too high,

And why,

Why do I love you?

There have only a been few, but every man I have loved in my life, even the ones I didn't love and was just "in love with" or "dating" or "seeing," was somehow involved with another woman. Most of the time, it was an ex-girlfriend or a baby momma that lingered around but who wasn't officially a girlfriend anymore. In some cases, they were actual girlfriends covered under a lie of being a past thing, or they were completely denied or simply not mentioned. Now, outside of the four really serious relationships I have had in my life, I have been around and dated quite a few guys, and it would be safe to say that in my twenties, I did have a certain type, but looking back at all of my experiences, I've been around and involved with different types of men. Some I like to call "boys," but a few were (older) men of various backgrounds. Nothing ever worked out for me, and in the end, I always lost to another woman. I used to wonder: Is this how relationships are? A constant battle between women for one guy? A continuous fight for attention? Naturally, I am someone who loves hard, and whenever I am into someone, I am really into them. Time and time again, I tried to ask myself if there was something wrong with me.

I was never sure why this kept happening to me—keeps happening to me. The average person, including a lot of my friends, would answer this by saying, "You pick the wrong men." But do you really pick who you fall for? I don't think I have ever done that, nor do I think I am capable of that because of the way I was raised and the way I love, which is genuine. I have always been heart driven and proud to be able to say that. I don't look at it as a bad thing in life, but in love, it's hurt me over and over again. Yes, I chose the men I wanted to date or have a little fling with, but I did not chose who I fell in love with. Why them?

CHAPTER 6:
Fallin'

IT WAS MY BIRTHDAY in April of 2012. I turned twenty-nine, and I will always remember this day as a turning point. Jay and I were still together, but I had been through so much in this relationship that I needed for things to finally get better. I didn't know how. But I was hoping for a nice birthday as a start.

This particular night, I had a gig on 26th and Broadway at this spot called Toshi's Living Room. It was a gig I shared with him. Looking back, Jay never *really* was my boyfriend except in my world. It lasted two years. He was the one I loved and wanted to be with. He was the one I would have given the world to. But he broke my heart one too many times that night. We sang our songs, and after we were done for the night, we sat down for a drink and a conversation, which we had dragged out for a while. Things had been extremely rocky for a while, and I needed to know whether or not he really wanted me (seems to be the story of my life).

Anyhow, it turned out that he didn't for many different reasons.

The other woman, our miscommunication, my little ways he could not stand, him being so damn anal, his weird self not knowing what he wanted in life, his issues overwhelming him so much he had no room for emotional commitment with another. I can confidently say that it had less to do with my flaws, even though they exist. I know for a fact that he knows he did not see what he had and took me for granted until I was gone—and that night was the beginning of me being gone.

He broke up with me, bluntly and direct as it can be. "It's over," he'd said, leaving me crying on the street, confused and hurt. Then, he left me standing, and when I followed him to the train station, while I was waiting on the same train as him, all of a sudden I was a stranger. We got on the same train, and he would not even look at me, like I had just killed his cat who he loves more than any human. At least, that's what I believe.

So, I got off at my stop without a goodbye.

It's weird because we had talked about breaking up before, but something that night told me that this was final.

As I started walking the block from 9th Avenue to 10th on 44th street, where I was living at that time, I was in tears and needed to tell someone what just happened.

This is what I call "the beginning. . . ."

I took my phone out of my bag and called Peter without hesitation.

I cried to him. I told him how much I was hurt by the way I had just gotten dumped. He consoled me and was the friend I needed in that moment. He told me I was a queen and that I should never let a man make me feel this low. I agreed, and it didn't take long for me to stop crying and feeling better . . . feeling strong, feeling like I would be okay.

Why did I call him? I am not so sure, but being that he was the one person that was friends with both Jay and myself, that he had been around us as a couple, had known our issues, and had been trying to fix things for us almost like our personal undercover therapist, I felt he understood what our relationship was about. I also had been in contact with him about doing a music group involving him and our other mutual friend Rob A. (which never happened). But anyways, at this particular point in time, he was a factor in my love drama with Jay. He was also someone who both Jay and I had grown to love hanging around. I never felt any kind of attraction toward him, never. I was so in love with Jay. I just thought Peter was a cool dude, very funny, and fun to hang out with . . . crazy, but fun. I had known him for a couple of years, but we hadn't been friends until the recent months leading up to this hurtful break up that I was now going through. All I ever knew of Peter was his reputation as "the biggest womanizer downtown"—always seen with different women. All the people in the club I worked at talked about him that way and confirmed to me that this reputation he had was not just a reputation; it was actually his life. Anyhow, I did not care what he was doing, or "who he was smashing," at all. I was too in love with Jay and was to no extent looking at Peter in that way. I had never even spoken to him more than hi and bye up until a few months prior to where we were now. . . .

But the next month or so, Peter and I spent a lot of time talking on the phone. We hadn't spent any time together, because I had been on tour the whole time. That's how he later gave me my nickname "World Tour." He would make jokes about me constantly being gone and traveling. By making those jokes, I could tell, he was anxious to have me back in New York.

We built our friendship, and I liked that. I still wasn't attracted to him in any way even at this time, but the more I talked to him on tour, the more I started liking his character, and I would look forward to getting those phone calls like every other day. Something about that connection we had made me forget about how much I was hurting over Jay. I believe it was May 2012, which was my last month of touring, I started writing down how I felt about my breakup every day.

For twenty days, I would write whether or not I cried that day, whether or not I was okay, and whether or not I had spoken to Peter. He hinted on Twitter towards my return to New York and started a countdown to my comeback, posting stuff like "8 days . . . ," "7. . . ." I found it funny, but I still did not feel like I wanted him in any kind of way but as my friend. A few days before I finally was coming home, I wrote in my journal, and what I wrote shocked myself. I wrote, "I left thinking about Jay, but I'm coming back thinking about Peter—wow!"

That was the start. . . .

Back in New York a couple days later, I felt nervous because I knew it wasn't going to be long until I would see Jay again since we still worked together, but shockingly, more than that, I was excited to see Peter. The night I landed, I dropped my bags, got dressed, and went downtown to this spot named the Groove where he was always at. This must have been sometime in late May 2012.

I don't remember what happened that night, but it was the beginning of summer and it wasn't only the season that felt great. . . . It was like I had come home to something. Something that made me feel good. My phone friend from the past few months was finally next to me, and I just knew this was going to be a good summer.

Over the next few weeks, we started hanging out a lot— sometimes during the day parkflow, and some days we had dinner, went to the movies, or just went downtown to take in all the live music that we both loved so much and hung out till daylight came up. We would listen to music we both enjoyed and just zone out. Without talking much, I felt connected. Everything he liked musically, I understood. Even if it was something I didn't love, I got why he did, and I loved that. I had a blast. I literally forgot about Jay whenever I was with Peter, but at times, I missed him, his crazy ass—the romance, his innocent-little-boy personality that came out only inside the four walls of his home. . . .

I felt like I could have helped him to become better and I failed. But then I remembered one of my favorite quotes, which reads, "You cannot save people; you can only love them." I had done just that, and I knew that the fault didn't lie in my hands.

During the next summer weeks, my friendship to Peter had grown into something like an infatuation, and every time we hung out, I got to liking him more and more.

I wasn't ready for anything more than a friendship, but the more I kept telling myself that, the more I wanted him around and close to me.

At least a month or two went by before we couldn't keep our hands off each other any longer. He drove me home while listening to my music (a song named "Touch" I had just recorded). This was a regular routine, but when we arrived at my spot on 44th street and 9th Ave. in Manhattan, instead of hugging me and watching me enter the building, he said, "I'm gonna come out and kiss you . . . *and then* go."

I just smiled, not knowing how to feel, but then I got out the car, and that is exactly what happened.

After the kiss, I went upstairs, alone and even more infatuated than I had become over the past couple of months. It was the most sensual moment, and I didn't expect that from him. I didn't expect it to feel the way it did. Him kissing me gave me a taste of how it would feel to make love to this man, and as much as I tried to deny it, I wanted just that. I couldn't wait for tomorrow, because I knew I would see him again.

Sure enough, the next day I got flowers. I'm not sure if his lawyer friend he was always with talked him into getting them for me or if it was his idea, but either way, I was happy that they both showed up at my house and surprised me. I was off work that day, but Peter still made his rounds to 44th Street just to see me. His boy kept making jokes about us two hooking up, and Peter kept making jokes about that not happening because of Jay.

I just went with the flow because I knew I was never going to *be* with this man. He was way too "out there" for me, way too much of a womanizer, and at this point, I didn't even know enough about him; all I knew was that it felt good having this much fun after I had been feeling so much pain from the previous relationship, which I did not care about much anymore . . . for now.

I never asked Peter whether or not he had a girlfriend, because, to me, it was obvious. He didn't. He couldn't have.

He had BOB (a bunch of bitches, as he liked to say), and I knew that—everybody knew that. He even had a song in which he listed a few of the girls names, and he started rapping it every time we talked about ex's. But again, I did not care, because what I was interested in was having a good time. And a friend.,

So, we continued. . . .

A few more days went by, and I got showered with more flowers and sweet messages. I really started feeling some way about him. *I get it now*, I said to myself. *This must be why all these women like him*. It wasn't just the charm he had and the fun energy that was so special; it was all the little things I didn't know about him that I got to see more and more every day—his views about art and politics, raising a child, or the music business. Every time we talked about life, I saw more and more of his wisdom. His intellect reminded me of my mom and where I came from, how I grew up, and I was not used to that way of thinking from a black American. How much he knew about things that interested me and how he spoke about them was so untypical, yet he was so "New York" so "cool" (and only a New Yorker will understand, or someone like me who has basically become one). The fact that he had been around, traveled, seen things outside of America, read books, and knew so much about jazz (the music my parents introduced to me) was a big deal! The way he listened to music and heard details in a song, the way he knew how to play any instrument we came across, the way he would use songs in his stories and tell stories in his songs, the way he would find humor in any and every situation, and how he simply enjoyed life was contagious. Everything about Peter was mesmerizing.

At this point in time, he was in the city like every day, and whenever I asked him where he lived, he would always answer, "The X! . . . and I got a spot in Queens." He would call me from Queens all the time saying he was with his five-year-old son. I told Peter I wanted to meet him, and he said he couldn't wait for me to.

I also knew he had Cory (his oldest), of course, whom I had known of since the Def Jam days—he was that sixteen-year-old genius that everyone talked about at Def Jam when my sisters and I were signed to them in 2006. At that time, I didn't know who Peter Gunz was, but now I knew.

I was not aware of any other kids. We just didn't talk about it. Not until later.

I was full of life when I was around him. He made me forget about any worries I had, and there were many. . . .

Anyway, it must have been June of 2012, and he wasn't holding back on touching me anymore. One night, as we were saying goodbye, he came in and walked me up the hallway, where we stopped halfway to make out. He always did make the first move, but it was me who asked if he wanted to come in this time. I felt him through his jeans as he put my hand down to his crotch. He shook his head and said, "Look what you did." That's when I pulled him inside. We all can imagine the rest. . . .

It was beautiful! It wasn't like we just had sex; it felt like making love. I guess I can describe it best as something like the "best of both worlds." It felt like his body was made for mine. He was so strongly built yet still touched me in the most sensual way and didn't hold back on his moves, which came with the right amount of roughness. . . . Ugh, I hated that it was so good! Cramped up in my tiny room, and with my roommates asleep, we had to be quiet and somehow manage to stay on my little futon. What a task. Yes, we both had been drinking a little, but after we finished, I felt completely sober and amazingly close to him. We passed out holding each other until the morning.

My experience with men in the past taught me that after you "do it," they lose interest. Not Peter. It was more like the opposite—we just wanted to be around each other more, we started hanging out even more, and we started doing it more and more.

I swear, we had the best time that summer. Months went by, and we had a blast! I was falling for him, and he for me! He kept saying it to me. I didn't; I was just flattered to hear him say it because I knew I felt the same. I kept my feelings to myself for now, however, maybe because the breakup with Jay was still fresh, maybe because I was scared to care too much and to show it because that can be a turnoff to some guys. I kept cool and just enjoyed our time together.

By the time fall came, we were a couple. I mean openly—to everyone—at least the people we mutually knew and all around downtown, where we would hang out most nights. Everyone knew we were, I guess I can say, *dating.* . . . It was obvious! And it didn't take long for Jay to catch on to what everyone already knew. I remember the day he called me out of the blue and asked if it was true. I couldn't lie. I didn't wanna lie. I knew it was going to crush him, but I did not care, only because he had crushed me months before. I was at a gig in midtown with an artist named K'naan whose band I was in at the time. I was about to go on stage, so the conversation with Jay was brief, but I kept it real. I remember the rest of this day was a back-and-forth phone tag—Jay calling Peter, Peter calling me, Jay calling me back, me calling Peter, Jay and Peter talking on the phone for hours. Eventually, Peter came clean, and later that night, he even let me eavesdrop on his and Jay's conversation on three-way. It was nuts. Crazy. Just a big old mess. Peter felt horrible. I could tell he really did. And that made me feel uneasy as well.

Jay was going insane trying to comprehend that his friend was fucking *his* woman (because I know that, even though Jay had left me months before, he still was considering me *his*, as so many men do after breakups). He definitely still had feelings for me. He felt deceived. He cried. He yelled. He would go from being calm to losing it, threatening Peter, to then saying he didn't believe this was happening to saying he could have me. I hung up after a few minutes. I felt like, even though this was about me, I had nothing to do with it—this was their issue which they should just sort out, or not. . . . I didn't care. I didn't feel like I had done anything wrong after what Jay put me through. He deserved just what he was getting; however, I wasn't happy that we were going through this. It was a story of its own that I don't want to go into any more detail about, because at this point, it was over with Jay. At least for me.

Funny how the tables turn.

Anyway, Peter was very comfortable with me in public, and that set me at ease about anyone else possibly still being there. . . . I didn't even ask. I knew at this point that his spot in Queens was shared with his baby-momma, the mother of their son JP. He always would say (verbatim), "It's at the end of the road with her," and in the next sentence tell me how much he had fallen for me. I didn't know what to make of that, but as much time as Peter spent with me, all these nights we spent together, weirdly, I just was not even concerned with her, because he was always with *me*. He never, ever spoke about her. He did speak of many other women he had recently been dealing with, and I was more jealous of those "affairs"—as I now know they were "affairs" . . . and there were a bunch! I had hung out with a couple of these women alongside Peter and Jay before so I knew them, some of them I had met just once, and others never, but Peter would always be very open about who he had "smashed," which, even though I didn't like hearing, I thought was cool.

Anyway, these girls started to get jealous, I guess because Peter had never been so "public" with them.

Everyone knew now that he was with Amina. At this point, when I looked at him, I was completely in love. It was weird because his character had made him beautiful in so many ways. I had always thought he was a good-looking guy, but he was never my type until I got to know him. The sex was amazing and got even better the more time passed, but what I loved most about Peter was that I felt like he understood me, as an artist and, more importantly, as a person. Men always initially liked me for my looks, which I guess is a normal thing, but I loved the fact that my looks weren't what had made him fall for me. It was me being who I am, who I had become and was so proud of. Me, who I loved myself.

As it got colder and winter came around, I started feeling possessive.

That's when things got complicated. . . .

CHAPTER 7:
Love is a Battlefield

AND AS THEY SAY, all's fair in love and war. I felt so close to Peter, but time would reveal that I was a soldier in the army fighting for a future that did not give me the privilege of certainty.

Here we were together and everyone knew, yet I didn't even dare to call Peter my "boyfriend." I just never expected that it would come to this. And I had told myself so many times that I would never date a man like him. But here I was, emotionally attached to this man, who had never brought me to his house.

Maybe in the back of my mind I didn't ask any questions because I was having the time of my life and I didn't want it to end. Maybe I felt that he was hiding a lot from me and didn't want to find out what it was because I was scared to lose what we had. I had gone from the most hurtful heartbreak to being so much in love, in such a short time. I found it amazing that this was even possible.

And even though I do think about my future, I, just like Peter, am someone who likes to live in the moment, not planning ahead or worrying about what could happen.

Nevertheless, at times, when I thought about this whole fling we had going on, I felt weird, like it was unwise of me to be indifferent to what this man's life was like outside of "us." I thought maybe I should step back . . . or maybe I should at least talk about it, and maybe I should realize that the chance of getting hurt was just too big.

Around this time, I wrote a song called "What It Feels Like." In the song, I sing about how I know love is probably not permanent, but I would never wanna miss the feeling. I talk about ours being real love and me never having felt that way before.

Something I know is that I never felt a love like this,

And no matter how it ends, i'd do it all over again.

Nothing can make me turn away from you, boy, no matter if I lose.

I'll be glad that I had you.

Basically, I knew that this situation was not everlasting and that something was going to happen and probably take all of this away from me.

There was one other thing that was bothering me, something that I had to face in the near future, which was the start of another process—applying for a work visa to stay in New York. I did not wanna leave again after having to do so many times before because my work permit had expired. I was employed and had never in my eleven years of being in the states overstayed or done anything illegal. I was always on point when it came to renewing my papers; however, it was a hassle and a headache. And there was traveling involved, plus the worry of having to "wait" months for approval again. I had been through this plenty of times with different record labels, different employers, and sponsors. (If you know anything about being a foreigner coming to America to work and make a career for yourself, you know that it is a freaking headache.)

Peter and I talked about everything! Thinking back, I must have bored him talking about all of my family in Germany and the people that I was close to who were so far away, but if I did bore him, he didn't show it; our conversations were the best. Peter was someone who made a lot of jokes all the time, so when he continuously said that we were going to get married so I could just stay and be there with him until I figured shit out, I would always laugh it off and say, "No we're not." He had been doing this for some time, and honestly every time he did, I thought that I would totally marry him if he was serious because we loved each other, plus it would mean that I wouldn't have to deal with the bullshit I was about to face. However, I never asked him how much truth there was to this "joke"; I just hoped that it could come true one day.

I don't remember where and how I spent the holidays this year, but it's clear to me now that he was with his "family" for Christmas as that is what he, still to this day, does every year. But for New Year's, he came to my job (where I was working) at midnight, and we celebrated all night! It was one of those "happy moments" for me, starting the New Year off with him right by my side. I actually remember having an argument about a girl in the club that night. It was complete jealousy on my end because this girl seemed to like him, and that made me insecure. I can now admit that; I was super jealous. LOL.

So, 2013 was here! The year of the craziness—I had no idea was going to unfold in the way that it did.

This whole marriage thing seemed to always come back up, and believe it or not, it wasn't me who brought it up; it was Peter. He had started telling people that he and I were getting married. It still seemed like a joke to me whenever he did, but the more he would talk about it, the more I looked at him as my future husband. That made me excited. I felt that, if he was really going to marry me, he was really mine. I still did not know a lot of things about his life and "situation" with baby-momma, though, and it was getting uncomfortable. But in my mind, I knew he would not talk about us like this if things were still serious with his baby-mom. Anyhow, instead of stressing him, I just waited. Since I was so excited, I did look into the process of getting married in New York and found that we needed to get a marriage license before we could actually get married. When I told Peter, he said, "When are we going?" I was shocked. I just smiled and replied, "Umm, next week. . . ." And guess where we were the following week? At the city clerk's office applying for a marriage license. I could not believe he showed up. I really could not believe this man was seriously going to marry me after we had dated no longer than six months—just like that! He was actually not joking the entire time. . . . Saying that I was excited would be an understatement!

Still, I didn't tell anybody, because even though it seemed real now, I had my doubts.

Valentine's Day was around the corner, and now that we were able to get married whenever we wanted, we just spontaneously decided to do it that week.

I remember saying to him on Valentine's Day, "Bring your passport because we're going in the morning." He replied, "Yup." He brought me flowers, and we had a beautiful Valentine's Day dinner. He was wearing a suit—I loved it when he did, and I think I had never seen him in one up until now. He just looked so damn good. I was not sure where he had been all day, but I think we all can put two and two together and know that he was with the other woman. But I was just happy we were spending time together and was looking forward to the night and our big day tomorrow!

This night I will forever remember as one of the craziest nights I've had! We got drunk as fuck, and I got high on a pill or two (something I had only done once or twice in my life). . . . We were faded! We ended up at our friend's apartment in Brooklyn, where we all started doing the craziest things with each other (me and Peter were the only ones who kept our hands and tongues between the two of us! I was way too possessive; I wasn't having any shenanigans with him and other women in the room, and he definitely wasn't having that either). We had sex . . . and lots of it . . . till the sun came up, and then, I realized, this is my wedding day! I looked at Peter passed out on the couch still in his suit, and I remember thinking, this man is about to be my husband . . . and so it happened. . . .

February 15, 2013

As I was trying to recover from this hangover, being the first one up, still at our friend's house, I realized that in all the excitement I had forgotten to bring my passport, and so without saying a word, I rushed back to midtown to pick it up. When I got back to Brooklyn, everyone else, including Peter, was still passed out!

I woke him and my close friend Ariana, who had agreed to be our witness the week before. I said, "Let's go! Are we going?" I didn't expect to get a yes, but both of them willingly got up and "got their shit together."

I had changed into a white-and-black mini dress that matched Peter's suit. We were all just super hungover and I think a bit in shock realizing what a crazy night we had

had, but we jumped in a cab and the destination was city clerk office downtown.

On the way there, we kept saying how crazy we were, and I don't think any of us realized that this was really happening. When we arrived, we got out the car, and Peter said he had to go to Walgreens real quick. Ariana and I waited for him outside, and when he came back, he had a bag with water and one-time toothbrushes, which I had never seen before in my life. This must have been something he was used to doing, but that didn't matter to me.

Everyone in the court was dressed really nice. There were kids and families; everyone was full of joy. It made me a little nervous, and I'm sure there was a lot going through Peter's mind as we were waiting. He was really quiet, but kept saying he was just really hungover. We took pictures, and then, finally, they called our name.

We went into the room. I remember my girl Ariana, who was holding my phone, kept laughing, and so did I. I just couldn't believe this was going down. It took all of six minutes. When Peter said, "I do," I could sense that his mind was spinning, but as he looked at me and it was my turn, I was reassured—this man loves me and this is why he was here. He wouldn't put himself through all of this if he didn't love me, so we had our first kiss as husband and wife. We were married. And I was happy.

We left the courthouse and grabbed something to eat at a sandwich spot around the corner (crazy, I know). Just my husband and I. We were holding hands, and he kept calling me Mrs. Pankey with the biggest smile on his face.

I knew he was going to go "home" after this long night of little sleep, and, while even writing this feels weird, I couldn't wait for my bed either, so we parted ways. He said he would see me later and couldn't wait to make love to his wife. Later that night, we did, and it felt amazing hearing him call me Mrs. Pankey while we you-know-what. . . .

Peter had only told very few people in his circle, but now that we had done it and I was his wife, he said to me, "We are married now; no more inappropriate shit with anyone!" He knew that a lot of men were always coming at me, even being disrespectful at times since I worked at a night club and my previous relationship was very private. Also, my personality is just always super friendly and nice, and a lot of men took that the wrong way and felt like they could come at me. Now that we were married, Peter said to me loud and clear, "Those days are over, and I'mma let niggas know." I loved it! Finally someone claiming me—something that Jay had never done. He slowly but surely told people that I was his wife. I remember the week after, he and I were at The Groove, one of our favorite spots in New York, and we went up on stage to jam with the band. After we were done doing our thing and I sang my part, Peter said into the mic, "Give it up for my *wife*, Amina." I was like, okay, I guess you're ready to really let niggas know! I was happy as ever. He kept telling me how everything felt different now that I was carrying his last name . . . how he was not going to tolerate anything, and even though he was always cracking jokes, the way he would introduce me as his wife to people made me just fall in love with him over again.

In March of 2013, a couple of weeks after we had become husband and wife, I had a show in East Village to celebrate the release of my new EP *I Am Part 1*. I invited a few of my friends, and Peter told me he invited some people as well. It turned out that half of the venue was filled with members of his family, most of whom I hadn't met. He had brought out all of his sisters and cousins, as well as their husbands, nephews, and kids to see me perform and to officially meet me, AKA, Peter's wife! I had not expected so many of them and was super excited but nervous. How would they react? Would they like me? Some of them found out that night that I was officially part of the family. But, because they all are amazing people, I was showered with support and love from the jump.

Even if some of them might have been confused, they didn't act like it and I was happy, and most happy because this made everything absolutely official. Finally.

Just like Peter let me know he wasn't comfortable with other men around me anymore, I wasn't comfortable with all the women who threw themselves at him and any situations he hadn't put closure to. Now that I was his *wife*, I felt entitled to know where he was, why he didn't pick up the phone, and who he was talking to. I know, sounds backwards, but it's how I really felt. This is where we started having problems, and I realized very fast that Peter was not really taking this whole thing seriously. Yes, he kept telling me I was the one he loves, I'm his wife, and he just needed to figure out this one situation with his "son's mom." It was getting on my nerves because I just needed him to take care of it already. Like, what was he waiting for? She didn't even know he got married, but at this point, being that everyone pretty much knew, I was just waiting on the day for her to find out so Peter wouldn't have no more excuses. . . .

Becoming his wife made me feel like he belonged with me, but our living situation was not even close to right. Peter kept telling me he was going to "handle it," talking about him living with baby-moms. He kept telling me how hard it was because of his son, whom he loves more than anything, which made my little considerate self feel sorry and not wanna rush him, and that he was going to move out when he was ready. But of course, this was where I was wrong.

In the meantime, I had found myself a spot in Brooklyn, so I moved from the shared home in the city into my first studio apartment ever. I told Peter, "This is for us." It was a tiny spot, but for me, it was an accomplishment. I'd never had my own spot, and I was excited despite the circumstances with my "husband." I was happy not having to be cramped up in one room with him anymore, and I told him to start bringing his stuff over, as he did. . . .

With Peter, I never knew how serious he was. He said a lot of things I now know he just said to say and didn't actually mean. One of them was saying I should get a tattoo of his name. I didn't hesitate, because I just loved him so much. I surprised him with a new "Mrs. Pankey" tattoo right after getting married, which he loved, or so it seemed. . . . He also told me I should change my name on Facebook from Schmahl to Pankey. I did. Without hesitation. The next day, one of his best friends RM, whom I worked with closely in the band, came up to me and expressed his feelings of that being "too much." I was like, "Excuse me?!"

Turned out, this friend had no idea we had gotten married. He thought I was playing a joke and that it could cause headaches for Peter at home because there were "children" involved.

I said, "Come again?"

"There are *kids*!" he said, "Two of them . . . it's two of them. Come on, Mina."

I was confused. All this time, I knew Peter had a son with this woman, but not two kids. I didn't say anything else, but, that night, Peter told RM that I was actually his wife now. He apologized and, in shock, congratulated me with a long hug. Later, I asked Peter if he had another child with his baby-mom, but he kept ignoring the question, which let me know that it was true. "What's his name?" I asked.

When Peter doesn't wanna answer a question, he, like so many other men, knows how to not answer it . . . and Peter didn't wanna answer that question. I let it go, but as we were hugged up in bed that night, out of nowhere, he said in a very serious tone, "His name is Milky."

I was glad he finally admitted and didn't lie about his child. He had just ignored the fact that this baby existed and he followed up saying, "Come on—I thought you knew. . . . I always say my *sons'* mom." Yes, he did say "his *sons'* mom," but how was I supposed to know there were two children? Anyway, the cat was out the bag, and I tried not to get too upset about it, but deep down, I will never forget how my heart sank to the floor finding out about a one-year-old after we had already been together for more than half of that year.

It became clearer to me every day that what I thought this relationship was, wasn't what he thought it was. Or, at least he was still very far away from looking at our marriage as something that should be respected. On the one hand, he expected me to be a wife and wanted me to act accordingly, but on the other hand, he would not see anything wrong with disappearing whenever he felt like it. After tying the knot, we spent the majority of nights together, making love and having fun, but the nights where I couldn't find him just seemed to be part of this dilemma I had gotten myself into.

The more I started expressing my feelings about that, the more we argued. I hated it. Sometimes, I was confused about what to do. Should I just accept that this was how it was, being that it was actually all my own fault? I was mad at myself. I mean, who gets married to someone they don't know much about? And who still lives with his ex? I blamed myself and, because of that, sometimes felt I didn't have the right to act up and demand things when I went into it not demanding much at all. The other side of me felt that I was being so good to him. I was taking this relationship seriously; I was loyal and was one hundred percent *his*. I was giving so much in this relationship, so why should I not get the same in return, especially when he expected me to be a "good wife"? Why shouldn't I have the right to ask him to be a "good husband"?

I loved Peter so much that I tried being patient. Maybe he really did just need some more time figuring shit out, and I didn't want to be a stressor in his overly stressful life. His happiness meant so much to me, almost more than my own. Living like this hurt me, but I just kept telling myself that time would tell whether he loved me as much as he said or this was all just a mistake. . . .

Knowing now that Peter actually was still in a serious relationship with his baby-momma, yet was married to me, was very uncomfortable when I thought about it, but whenever I would just focus on him and me, there was nothing but happiness and the greatest of times. It was that kind of love that I had never felt before. All these times I had been in love before this were unimportant, and even though I did love my past boyfriends, it never was a love this deep. I knew what it felt like now. But of course, it was a reality that I was in a crazy situation here, and I just could not wait for the day this type of living would come to an end. I hoped he would just come clean and stop living this double life. I also feel that deep down he wanted this "secret" to come out but didn't wanna be the one to break the news and wanted to wait for "the right time," which he kept saying to me, but I think anyone would agree that the right time would have been before we said, "I do." He just had gotten himself so deep into this that it seemed like the longer he waited, the harder it got for him to reveal the truth to his baby-mom, and the more he wished he wouldn't have done what he did.

He never ever expressed that to me, but I could feel that this was how he felt. I'm not a fool, so I knew that at times it must have been really hard for him and he must have felt like, "Damn, what have I done?"

One night, he and I met up with his boy Richie D who was filming a scene for a reality show (in it's 3rd season) in a restaurant on 46th Street. They had asked Peter to be in the scene, and he brought me on set. I stayed behind the cameras, as no one knew who I was, but I was excited for Peter. They even asked me if I wanted to be in the scene, I guess as something like a seat filler, but I declined. It seemed like Peter knew everyone, and we hung out for a while after they wrapped the scene. He told me he is going to do another one the following week, and this is how it all started. . . .

He got to talking to the producers about his life, and the next thing I knew, they wanted to meet me. Everything went super fast.

I had watched the show before a few times and knew that it was a lot of craziness and drama going on between cast members, especially the women. I knew Peter had told the producers that I was his wife, but he had also told them he was still in a relationship with the other woman. Yes, she was the other woman to me. Peter and I were an item. He was my husband. We did things together every day. I knew that I didn't have him all the way, but what I also knew was that what we had was real. I was aware that this woman was going to be part of the show if we ended up doing it, and something in me said this might be a good thing; it would be a definite way to finally put everything on the table. More so, I was thinking about what this could mean for me, being that I had nothing going on with my music. Yes, I had recently released my first solo EP, but no one knew, nobody cared, and nobody bought it. I was super proud of it, and I felt that if I ended up on TV and millions of people saw me, I might gain some fans and it could help me on my journey as an indie artist. That was the main thing that made me wanna do this show.

I remember going to meet some of the production heads at VH1. I sat down at a big round table with about eight other people, some of whom I knew and some were introduced to me, but they all seemed to be very important in this whole thing.

They started asking me questions about my life and about Peter and me. They asked if I knew of his baby-momma, and I said, "Yes, I do, but I'm his *wife*! We are together, and we love each other. . . . She is the 'other woman,' and I need her to understand that Peter loves me. She might think they are still together, but Peter wants out." This is really what I believed at this time and place. Silly me . . . because some time had passed and this woman still had no idea about her "man" being married to someone else. The feeling that Peter cared about her a lot more than he showed me kept coming over me. I knew he didn't wanna hurt her, and although I was confident in what he and I had, every now and then I felt that this was not going to end well.

The more I spoke, the more the producers of the show seemed to be intrigued by this story. I told them about my musical history, my record deals, my group Black Budda-fly, having been in the music industry, and all the things that I had learned and that led to me doing my own thing. They told me to sing a little, and I gave them an acapella, the hook to my new song I had just written about Peter, "What It Feels Like." They loved it!

After the meeting, I was excited; I saw myself finally doing what I love in front of an audience, instead of the four walls of my home or on my YouTube channel with a few thousand viewers.

So, going into this, I was not nervous—I felt strong, confident, like I'm gonna show these hoes who I am and they're gonna love me. Oh, was I wrong. . . .

CHAPTER 8:
A Thin Line between Love and Hate

S O, HERE WE WERE, on set to film our first scene for *the show,* season four.

My bedroom was the location, and the entire production crew was set up to film Peter and I at home. There were a ton of people, and even though it was weird, being that I've always been a very open person, letting the cameras into my life was not uncomfortable at all. This was a regular morning, the alarm going off, Peter jumping up to head "home" to take his son to school, what he did every morning. They captured me being sad that he was leaving, a little upset even. I wasn't happy with this routine, only seeing him after he had taken care of his "family" and spent time in his other "home." But I also felt wrong and selfish telling him to stay with me. I expressed how I wished things were different, but I also let him know that I loved the commitment he had as a father. What really bothered me was that I knew going to his son also meant he was going to the other woman.

No part of me was concerned or even thinking about how my actions and words could come across on TV at this point; I was just being myself, and I really was just excited about the fact that I was doing something else with my life other than sing at a night club and releasing music for my own pleasure. I was not at all thinking about what kind of stress all of this was going to bring to my relationship and my life in general . . . though I *really* could have known!

As our life continued to play out in front of the cameras, I could sense Peter's anxiety about the day of truth. He knew it was coming, even though he did tell me to not mention us being married whenever cameras were rolling. It upset me, but I knew that it was only a matter of time before this secret was going to be out! So, I continued being patient. He kept me quiet and content by saying, "It's all gonna come out soon anyway." I knew this was fact! I knew he wasn't lying, but who would have thought it was going to be me delivering the big news to his baby-momma (who at this point had filmed a few scenes with Peter as well).

I remember the day because I don't think I had ever felt so disrespected before.

The producers came to film me at a gig in Brooklyn, and after I finished singing, I sat down at the table with my potential new managers Richie D and his partner. We got to talking business, but it wasn't long before we got interrupted by the "other woman" herself. I was a little uncomfortable simply because there was so much I knew that she didn't. So much I knew about her "boyfriend" that she had no idea I knew.

I let her speak—for a while—and she told me she knew what was going on between "her man" and me, how they had been together for years, and I shouldn't act like I wasn't aware of that. Well, truth is, I wasn't. I had no idea how many years they had been together. Yes, by now, I knew he never broke up with her, but what I also knew at this point, and what I thought in that moment, was he is my husband and we are madly in love; he still lives with you, but he wants out and just doesn't know how to end it for good.

As we kept talking, I remember thinking that I had never felt so disrespected in my life. I thought I was going to have the situation under control, but I didn't. She completely took control in this conversation, and it felt like she had most definitely rehearsed what she was going to say to me, something I didn't do. I couldn't get a word in and felt I was being talked down to like I'm some piece of shit and not of any value.

It reminded me of the situation I had gone through years before with that ex manager who continuously talked down to me and wanted to make me feel like I was nobody.

I ended up walking out on him and the record deal he had gotten my group back in the day. I do not play games, I do not pretend, and I never wanna put on an act for approval. At least, that is what this situation with my manager at the time taught me. Freedom was my choice back then, and it's been my choice ever since.

I'm not witty with my words like a lot of other people; I'm a thinker and a writer, an observer, not a talker. So, I've always felt like I was being trampled on in a heated conversation. I never felt the other party was smarter than me, but they were certainly more trained, more prepared. I've been a loner ever since my early teenage years, an introvert, someone who keeps to themselves a lot. That doesn't make me dumb; actually, my mind goes places that have no words.

Anyway, back to the story, I felt bullied, and this woman was making it seem like I was interfering in her life and relationship that was so perfect. At one point, her words started to blur, and my mind started spinning. I felt so many emotions; I was not going to have her continue to make me feel like I was some piece of shit when I felt I was the opposite. "I am a queen, and I love myself," I said to myself. "I have been through a lot, and you're trying to bring me down? No. I am about to tell you who the fuck I am."

And so I whipped out my driver's license that I had just gotten renewed, with my brand new last name on it, a name she knew very well, her "man's" last name—*Pankey*.

I slammed that shit on the table and said, "I *am* his *wife.*" Cameras were rolling, and I'm almost certain that that is why this woman reacted by slapping me across my face. Out of the blue, I just felt something more like a punch. I was ready to fight back because, trust me, my niceness is never to be taken for weakness!

I've never been a fighter in that sense, but I ain't scared of one, and I would not back down if it came down to it.

In this case, everything just went super fast and security separated us before a split second went by. Shocked at what had just happened, I was relieved that the secret was out! That night, Peter came home to me, which came unexpectedly. Yes, he should have always come home to his wife, but fact was that he didn't. So, it made me feel even better that he was around me this night when the other woman just had learned such insane news and probably needed him more.

Before this encounter, I had no negative feelings towards this woman. I had no idea what kind of person she was and, rather, felt sorry about what was happening in her life behind her back. However, after this day, my feelings changed, not only because I got physically attacked, but more so because of the way she spoke to me, talked down to me, and had zero respect for a fellow woman that was being lied to. She talked as if I was to blame for this mess. And yes, I knew of her at this point, but exactly that was the reason I wanted her to know! She wasn't aware of my position; she thought I was an irrelevant hoe who was trying to break up her "happy home." I wanted to let her know about the love between Peter and me. She deserved to know that I was not *only* smashing "her" man! With that said, I did not feel that it was fair how I was being talked to and felt backed into the corner. Which triggered my act. Why was she allowed to tell me so aggressively about the depth of her relationship with Peter, but I wasn't? Why was she allowed to get loud and start yelling, but not me? And why, when she expressed that he belonged to her, wasn't I supposed to express what I believed, which was that he belonged with me? Was it because she was there before me? I didn't find that relevant in this moment, because, fact was, Peter had let this go so far that our hearts were in this, or at least I can say that for myself.

After this day, all hell broke loose for Peter at "home." That's what he would tell me every day, and it only made sense. I believed him when he told me how nasty things would be. I remember the day he called me devastated about all his clothes and stuff being gone, cut up, ripped apart, or damaged. "I have nothing," he kept saying. It was the saddest voice I had ever heard him speak in.

"You have the clothes here, and you have me," I said, trying to make him feel better. I'm not so sure if that worked, but he did spend more time with me at my house, and I don't know why, but I just wanted to be his support in this time. Having more of an understanding of the history and depth of their relationship and feeling and hearing that this was going to finally really be it, I knew it wasn't easy for him, because obviously he loved this woman. So, I put my anger towards Peter to the side. Thank my parents for raising the nice human being that I am. He had always said that I am his escape, the getaway from the BS. I wanted to be that, especially now. I wanted to be the wife that helps him through this, rather than another woman who adds on to the stress.

Honestly, I never wanted to leave. I wanted to be there for him. Even more now than before. Yes, I was mad about the fact that he had downplayed the entire situation with that woman, but knowing how he felt for me and him continuing to make me feel like I was who he wanted kept me wanting to stay. If I would have been a mistake, this was the time he would have realized that and stopped what he was doing with me. Once and for all. This was the moment he should have fought for the other relationship . . . with actions. Actions like leaving me alone. Not actions like making love to her. If it crossed his mind, I don't know, but he sure did not say anything that pointed to him letting me go, nor did his actions say we needed distance. In fact, he came up with this line, which I ended up using in one of my favorite songs, "If you leave me, I'mma kill you!" It was a joke, but I always smiled when he said it to me.

Through the craziness that was happening, I felt loved. And as he continued to ask me to "just bare with him," I did because I knew, just by how this all happened, things weren't going to be right overnight. I again needed to give him more time, and though I hated it, I felt that he was worth it. I still had so much hope for us during this phase.

The only thing that really bothered me was that he was not showing his love for me anywhere the other woman could see it. I consoled myself by saying that his guilt wouldn't let him do that to her. He said he doesn't want to "turn the knife," and I understood, or at least tried to. Was I comfortable with it? No. Was this acceptable? No. But was there really something I could have said to change it? Peter had become a married man overnight, and even though I felt like sometimes he didn't really wanna be married to me, I knew that our love was real. He had chosen to continue loving me; did I really wanna make him "prove it" to the world when I knew this?

I should have. But I always felt like I was asking for too much because this was not a normal situation. This was extreme. This was different. Sometimes, when I would say how I felt, he would respond, "I'm here, and I married you. What more do you want? This should let you know where I wanna be. I have two kids there, and this is hard." I knew it was hard.

I always wondered what the conversation and interaction would be like between him and his baby-momma now that things were out in the open. I would play out all possible scenarios in my mind and it would drive me crazy. The only thing he would tell me was "it's all fucked up!" but obviously I knew that wasn't accurate. When the show finally aired six months later, I got to see only a tiny glimpse of it, but it shed some more light on how much he was still lying to me. . . .

I always got disappointed with Peter. And especially now, as the world was watching, it became harder and harder. I really started understanding that I was the one who had been foolish. Not being concerned with what else was going on, only because I was confident in what Peter and I had, was crazy. I knew it was.

Being labeled a side piece or home wrecker was another thing I should have seen coming, but I did not expect it to get so overwhelming. I really didn't. Honestly, I never thought about what people might think of me before they started having very verbal opinions and bashed me left and right for who they thought I was. Why hadn't I been concerned? Because I sincerely felt that I hadn't done anything wrong. All I had done was listen to my husband, trusted him, and believed his lies. But was I really responsible for a family being broken? I didn't think so. And I still don't think so today.

Around this time, when I felt the world was against me, when I was receiving so much hate and negativity, and when I realized there was still so much more there between Peter and his "ex" than I thought before, I would tell him, "I want you to do what your heart wants." I told him this on many occasions. And I meant it. I would literally tell him, "You should go back to her." He wouldn't. Maybe he couldn't, but he would only tell me that he didn't want that. It all was possible. Again, I would make myself crazy trying to figure it out.

When the day came and I found out that they were still sleeping together, well . . . that I was hurt would be an understatement. I cried waterfalls because of how much it hurt, but not because I was shocked. Obviously, this had crossed my mind before it got thrown in my face, and I always thought that if they were still doing it, I would not wanna be here no more; I would tell Peter that's it and move along. . . . But how many women forgive a cheating man, or even husband, when they find out the first time? Most women have been through it, and while there might be bold ones who are able to turn off their heart and emotions, women who love hard will give a second chance. Because I am one of these women, and all of this was televised, I was now not only a horrible person, a bitch, a whore, and a homewrecker—I was also dumb. The amount of times I had to hear those words in reference to me is insane. I was not ready for it. It tore me down in the beginning. But luckily, I can say *only* in the beginning. It all changed with time.

I understood that the reason I stuck with Peter was something these people wouldn't see. So, when I would get upset and feel hurt by the comments and judgements of strangers, it never lasted. I would think about the person I am. I would think about how loving my family is and where I came from, how I was raised, how much I've achieved in becoming *me*, whom I was so proud of. I started to understand that they didn't know the real me, but I do. That's how I came to write a song entitled "The Real Me."

I try to do my best and keep being strong, despite everything that they got to say,

Trying to wake up a monster that doesn't exist, 'cause I am an angel, angel flown away

Into my own world, where I can't hear or feel or see anything but my identity

And the real me.

CHAPTER 9:
The Sweetest Thing

AND, NO MATTER how weak you may feel, the power of love restores and heals.

Months went by, and I was on a rollercoaster ride with this relationship. Going from being totally fed up and thinking this would never be what I'd envisioned and deserved, that we were just not going to work (like everyone else thought), to saying and feeling that I didn't ever wanna be without him again in this life and we would make it through this! (Fuck what they think. . . .) It would literally change like night and day every other week. The fights we had were extremely intense but so was the love making and the fun we had when we let go of the outside world's influence and the drama that was happening. "I could never let go of this," I would think in those times.

However, these good times never lasted. And it's crazy to say, but because I knew that, I would appreciate them so much more.

In December of 2013, after we had basically just become famous overnight and had almost wrapped filming our first season for the show, a reunion show was scheduled to be taped right before Christmas. I did not know what to expect. I knew that the entire cast would meet in one setting during these "reunions" and dredge up everything that happened during the season. They were always explosive and emotional. I was definitely anxious to get it over with.

A couple of weeks leading up to the taping, Peter and I were just not in a good place. I was upset. I felt that he didn't wanna play "happy house" with me because this event was coming up and that would mean he would have to do so right before the eyes of the other woman. I felt that he wanted us to break up because of the public perception. I was mad. Actually, I didn't speak to him for a few days. As emotional as I am, feeling like we might really be done this time, I was not well. But I also felt off physically.

I remember having a club hosting the week before in Virginia. I took my friend A with me, and as I was getting ready in my hotel room that night, she started asking me about Peter and me. I completely broke down crying telling her about the messed up situation. . . . "And I think

I might be pregnant," I added. I had been feeling sick and weak for a few days, and my period hadn't come. With the awareness I have over my body, I always know when something is different, and I just felt it. Yet, I wasn't sure. It was definitely very possible thinking of how much we had been fighting and making up, which always included making love! I had a lot of champagne that night at the club because I was so depressed about Peter. When I came back home the next day and the feeling continued, I bought a pregnancy test, but I did not dare to take it. I think it was because I already knew the result and was scared. I envisioned myself taking the test and my reaction to it being positive; I knew it would make me cry and I didn't wanna cry. I had been crying so much lately.

If I was really pregnant, I couldn't even be happy about it. I wasn't even sure that I could stay with Peter. And this would just be bad! But the night before the taping of the reunion, I just had to know if what my body was telling me was true. To no surprise, the test was positive. And to no surprise, I broke down on the floor of my Brooklyn studio apartment. No Peter in sight. (We were still fighting. . . .)

I picked up my phone to text him that we needed to talk, but when I looked at our most recent texts, I changed my mind because of how nasty they were. I texted the other closest person to me instead. My twin sister Jazz.

She was the first and only person I told that I had life growing inside of me. First, she was excited, but when she heard about how messed up the whole situation was, I guess she could feel a little bit of how I was feeling. That is what twins do, and we have done it all our life. Abortion was not an option. Not at thirty years old, being a woman who wanted kids. Not after having had one before in my life (eight years before). The circumstances being what they were, I was not going to consider abortion. As a matter of fact, I had promised myself to never ever do that again. So the next move was to figure out how to tell Peter.

"Should I tell him now, or should I wait till tomorrow at the reunion?" I asked Jazz.

Knowing how Peter liked to keep things on the low with me, she said, "Do it tomorrow."

I agreed. . . . I was still so angry at him from our most recent fights. And I knew that if I had told him in private, he would have forbid me from speaking of it to anyone until it was impossible to hide anymore. Yeah, he had that kind of power over me. But I didn't wanna live that way anymore. I took the positive test, closed the cap, and put it in the bag that I had packed with all my stuff for the big day.

All of a sudden, I started feeling even more sickness kicking in. It wasn't just morning sickness; it was a full day of sickness and nausea that I was feeling times ten now. Just horrible.

No matter how messed up this was, I kept thinking that it was supposed to happen. I was supposed to have this man's baby, and I was supposed to have it now. It wasn't an accident. I mean, we weren't trying to get pregnant, but we also weren't trying not to.

The next morning, I got picked up super early to get ready for filming. Peter and I had briefly talked about just not being nasty to one another even though things might be shaky right now. We also had to perform together on this day. A song I wrote about him and our love entitled "Don't Wanna Be Right." He was definitely uncomfortable performing with me in front of his other woman, whom he felt had been hit the hardest in the past year. It might have been true. However, I also hadn't been spared from too much hurt. And I always felt that he ignored that or thought I shouldn't complain, because, after all, I am his wife and he ended up with me.

I remember Peter continuously asking me if I was okay on this day. It must have showed that something was wrong, and it seemed like he could feel it. I was scared. Scared of his reaction. I had this big secret that no one knew and I was about to shock everyone, so of course I was nervous. That's why I waited till the very end of the day to show him the pregnancy test in front of everybody!

He was not happy that I chose to expose such news on television as opposed to in private. He was not happy at all. He reacted by being mute, putting his head down, and then walking off stage where he, the host, his baby-mom, I were sitting.

The production stopped for commercial and, outraged, producers came running to me asking why I had not let them know this information beforehand.

I had expected Peter to be upset, but seeing him walk off stage the way he did and not even say a word to me made me realize that I had just disappointed him big time. Despite all the disappointments he had put me through, I still never wanted to do him like that. I believe in treating people the way you wanna be treated and not treating them how they treat you!

I was wrong. When production asked me to leave the stage because Peter wanted to come back out and only talk to his baby-mom, I felt extremely humiliated. This was one of the moments that made me so confused because, in these moments (and I say "moments" because they continued happening), the way I knew Peter felt about me just was gone. I would think, "Was I wrong about him?" I witnessed him cry to the other woman from backstage, saying how sorry he was for everything and that he would leave her alone to never cause any more pain. It was the most hurtful thing I had been through up until this point. I was just not important in that moment. I did not matter. Only she mattered. I was dismissed. X'd out of the occasion. I was pregnant, and I was hurting. This wasn't a good combination.

Coming back home that night, I just felt like I was never going to speak with Peter again. I felt like this was going to be a horrible Christmas, and I'd just be sitting in my apartment alone and depressed. I wanted to get out, for nothing but to get out of here! Be gone! I couldn't stop crying. I turned my phone off. I could not talk to anyone. I fell on my couch, opened my laptop, and started browsing for vacation getaways. Far away I wanted to go. Five hours later, I was at the airport, alone, with one small bag. Feeling extremely sick, I hadn't eaten anything. I felt weak, but I knew I had a long flight ahead of me, and I just couldn't wait to fall into the airplane seat and pass out . . . as I did.

I woke up in Honolulu, Hawaii, about twelve hours later. I had a short layover to go to another island called Kauai. Breathing the air and the ocean, feeling the heat, and knowing that I was just so far away from everything and no one knew, I felt a little better. But what had happened in New York still kept running through my mind over and over and over again. After checking in to my hotel, I went to my room, closed the blinds, fell on the bed in my clothes, and cried myself to sleep. The next seven days I spent pretty much in silence—taking walks, staring at the ocean, sleeping, driving through the mountains, and thinking about this baby that was in my belly. I kept my phone off for the majority of the trip but turned it on every now and then to see who tried to find me. My family was worried, my friends in New York were looking for me. Peter had gone to the house and found in my laptop that I had left. . . . The only text I got from him read, "I love you and my unborn child." I wasn't sure what to make of it. I just knew I loved him too, despite the pain he was causing. So I told him that and turned my phone back off right after.

I had never spent Christmas by myself. Seeing all the families—fathers, mothers with their kids on holiday in my resort—made me miss mine. A lot. . . . I called my mom. It was the only phone call I made that week. Surprisingly, she knew I was pregnant. I guess everyone knew. It had only been a few days since my announcement, and it hadn't even aired on TV yet, but I guess blogs had gotten the information and spread the news.

"Everything will be okay," my mom told me. As always, she supported wherever I was at with my feelings and just wanted to make sure I was taking care of myself and following my heart with any decisions that lay ahead.

I will forever remember this trip as an extremely painful but beautiful getaway. I would sit for hours and let go of my fears and worries and just breathe. It was just what I needed. I also believe it enhanced the connection I now have with my daughter. She was with me the entire time, and, yes, she was only a fetus but I believe she felt me as crazy as it sounds.

I knew now that, no matter what happened with my life and my relationship drama, I was going to be a mom. It was real. I just couldn't imagine what it would be like, but I always wanted kids and this, after all, was a beautiful thing.

At the same time, it was a scary thought. I was so me-driven. Yes, loving Peter had definitely taken the focus off myself and put it on him a lot, but I had never neglected my needs and wants as far as my lifestyle. I was aware that having a baby would completely change it. But I accepted it. I thought about my mom and how she had completely devoted her life to her daughters, never left our side, and put all her desires, wants, and needs off so she could raise us and, most of all, be around us. I wanted to be that kind of a mom, a mom that has a bond with her child. I believed in doing things the way nature had proclaimed: Breast-feeding, co-sleeping, always having your baby by your side (at least as an infant). However, I also didn't wanna lose my dream and give up on what I had been born to do. There are so many women who do both, so why couldn't I? I was confident that I would manage to balance career and baby and become a "supermom." I had done so much, traveled a lot, partied even more, and found myself in my twenties; even though this situation was a mess, I felt this, if ever, might just be the right time. Being pregnant by the man I love and am married to might not be the worst thing in the world, even if Peter and I were over. This is what I would tell myself.

A positive thought followed by a negative one, my feelings were all over the place.

The last few days of this trip, I was anxious to get back home to New York. This was such a beautiful place, if not one of the most beautiful places I had ever been to, but I was just not able to enjoy it as my sickness had gotten worse. I was ready to face what awaited me. Tons of texts and phone calls from people I had ignored the past week.

Going back to work and seeing Peter. Because, no matter what was happening, now that I was pregnant, he was a permanent figure in my life.

When I was finally back in New York, he made me understand that he wasn't mad I was pregnant; he was mad about the fact I kept it from him and exposed it while cameras were rolling. He had awaited me, and being that I was so vulnerable, I fell into his arms and let him console me. This was my husband, the person I was closest to. I just couldn't help but let him catch me as I was falling. Anything to make me feel better. I had never been this low, and him kissing my belly and telling me that he loved us, definitely did.

A few months later, we finally moved in together. He kept assuring me that this pregnancy sealed the deal on the other situation being over for good. At this point, I really didn't trust it anymore, but I just couldn't help but wanting to try.

Even though I knew he didn't have much of a choice but to completely move out of his old "home" as his baby-mom had found a new place for her and her kids (minus Peter!), I was happy about the fact that we finally were going to officially live together.

He didn't have to move in with me . . . but he did. He didn't have to continue anything with me if what happened at the reunion made him realize how much he had messed up; he could have just decided to be there for his child and, again, fight for the other relationship, but he didn't. And if he did, it wasn't enough, because he was here, with me.

As my belly grew, my love for my child grew by the day. Feeling her move inside of me made everything so real. Springtime was here, and I finally stopped having morning sickness and felt better. We started filming another season of the show, and I was working on music in our new home studio that Peter and I had set up at the apartment. One of the first songs I worked on was a song to my daughter called "Never Gonna Be Alone," which Peter jumped on, and we later shot a video for.

And I'm never gonna be alone, never gonna be alone again

You got my back I can feel it, don't even need to see it,

Though I can't wait to see your face.

I know we'll be forever one, forever one,

And I'm never gonna be alone again,

I'm here and you're with me, this love I got in me is never ending,

And I'll never be alone again.

I didn't mind that Peter wasn't home all the time, because I liked my space. I needed it to be creative and work on my own music like I used to when my sister and I were living in Brooklyn. All this craziness had set me back a little, and I wanted to get back into my music zone that I felt like I had neglected.

However, when Peter wouldn't show up at all, I was not happy. I knew this is what he did. He had been doing this as long as I'd known him. I didn't think it was going to change just because his name was on the lease now. But it still made me feel some kind of way. Not good. I did not want to accept sharing him with other women, but here I was. Even if I didn't know of other women, I definitely knew of one other woman. The dilemma now was that carrying his child had made me feel even more connected to him. I hated arguing. I hated it with a passion. It was draining. Often times, I thought about why we fought so much. Then, I would look at myself and think, *if I don't complain, there won't be an argument.* I tried that, but it's just not for me to "play games" or "be strategic" when it comes to matters of the heart. I only know one way to be, and that is to be real! Always been that way and always will. I felt that if he didn't do the things he did, I wouldn't have to complain, and there wouldn't be an argument. It was clear that I wasn't at fault here, but in a way, and I knew this, I was stupid for complaining about something that I knew he had been doing forever. Being down, sad, and mad just made him not wanna be around me even more. But how could I not be? It was because of him that I felt this way. . . . I was going in hopeless circles.

And not knowing what to do, I was hurting a lot during my pregnancy.

Sometimes, I cried so hard that I felt guilty because of the baby inside of me. I would talk to my baby and apologize for the stress I felt like I was causing by being so emotional. Like that would help—smh. Crazy.

Leaving him was on my mind more than ever during this pregnancy, and, as they watched, I know the world was screaming, "Just leave him!" But it was just not that simple. It never is when you really love someone.

We had just taken a step forward. Everything was finally coming together but at the same time falling apart. Every time I was at my breaking point, Peter would do something to mend my pain, and it was not always sex. Most of the time, they were bolder gestures like bringing his sons over, even though their mother didn't want them around me or taking me to New Orleans to spend time with his two daughters, whom the other woman had never been around. He simply gave me his time and loving devotion, which was all I ever wanted. I thought that, if I gave up now, I would have regrets—and I don't ever have regrets. If I continued living this way, it meant I was accepting it, and I didn't want to do that either.

I never felt like I needed Peter. Or any man for that matter. After having been on my own in so many situations and always somehow coming through by myself, plus just being an independent kind of woman, I never felt like I wouldn't make it on my own, but it was no secret that I was stuck on him. I just wanted him so bad. He was my addiction.

It is a well-known fact that having a baby doesn't keep a man, and I had always known that. My mom had taught me better than that. However, having a baby might make you wanna try harder for someone you really love, and so I did. . . .

CHAPTER 10:
Throwing Stones at a Glass House

WHEN YOU LOVE HARD like me, you need the negative to outweigh the positive to put an end to a situation. I definitely did. In this case, as much as I was going through it, the love I had for my husband and our connection was bigger. Bigger than the pain. I had to keep on fighting for this relationship.

Yeah, I might have been naïve at times—focusing tenaciously on the good things when he was doing so many bad things—but I kept fighting, not because I was blind to what was going on, or because I thought he was going to change for me what he never changed for another woman he loved, but because I could still take it. In a weird way, I also felt that the more BS we would go through and overcome, the stronger it made us as well as my desire to make it work.

What sense does that make when he didn't want it to work as much as I did, you may ask? To me, it made sense because, through all the pain I was enduring, I needed to follow my heart, even if it wasn't "the right thing to do." It was my choice to live with all of this stress. I'd rather that than to leave, live stress free but feel the pain of missing him. It's not stupid. I call it personal preference. I was living in the moment, not being focused on the future. Right now, I wanted to take the hits of disappointment if I could have him around me, even if it was on his terms and not as much as I loved. Most people looking at it from the outside, however, felt I was the "dumbest bitch on the planet." Whether they thought I believed his lies or I didn't think he loved his ex or I thought he was "all mine," I don't know. Whatever it looked like on TV, I continued to be labeled stupid and brainless. There was so much hate coming my way, and it just wouldn't stop. Again, knowing myself saved me during this time. But wherever I went, and especially wherever Peter and I went together, there was nothing but love and people going crazy because they felt like they knew us from watching our lives on TV. We couldn't go anywhere without being stopped for pictures, and sometimes, they would chase us down the mall just to get a hug or a handshake, like we were celebrities. In those moments, I realized we actually were.

Pregnancy was draining and felt like eternity, but one of my favorite moments was finding out the sex of our baby. We were having a girl. I knew I was much more excited than Peter because he already had daughters . . . as well as sons. He had been through this many times before. Yet, he showed his excitement whenever he did make it to the doctor's office with me. It was weird for me to be set on having a girl when they would tell me that they could not determine one hundred percent. "It looks like a girl," they said, and when I would ask how certain they were, they told us seventy-five to eighty percent.

Back in the day in 1983, when my mom was pregnant with Jazz and me, they had told her one of us was a definite boy. They had been wrong. I know this is over thirty years ago, but I would sometimes wonder what if they were wrong about my baby girl, not that it would have mattered; I would have loved my boy just the same, but I always saw myself having girls when I thought about kids. I actually used to tell guys sarcastically I had two daughters when they asked me if I had kids, just as a joke to see their reaction. Funny how life works. . . .

Anyway, here we were looking for girl names. Peter was the first to throw out suggestions, but I wasn't sold on any at first. One day, we were having dinner at one of our favorite spots called the Olive Tree Cafe in West Village, where you can draw on the tables with white chalk while waiting on your food. As we were talking about the baby, Peter picked up a piece of chalk and wrote, "Cori."

"You have a Cory," I responded a little confused

"Yeah, but with a Y," he said.

I loved the sound of it, and I loved the idea of having a unisex name and having her named after her older brother and father (Peter's middle name is Cory as well). The fact that this name ironically was also the name of one of my exes didn't bother me one bit; I knew once I had this baby girl and was looking at her, that name was only going to be affiliated to her. And that is exactly what happened!

I continued performing and playing live shows while pregnant. It was one of the more rewarding things I did, as viewers had recognized the real artist that I am and, wherever I would go to sing, admired my talent. This was a good thing. This had been the main reason why I wanted to be on TV—making people aware of me as an artist. It worked. Even if many people said my artistry was being overshadowed by the drama, I had seen a huge change in my independent music sales as well as my fan base. It was growing, and that made me feel good. I had music out already, but my releases were always EPs with only a few songs on them, and I felt that it was time for a full album. I started this process while pregnant. I was still an indie artist, so I did everything under my terms, on my own time, and to my liking. I wasn't rushing it; I just created. Though I was in a totally different place in my life now, it sometimes reminded me of those times in Brooklyn where it had all started. . . .

But now it was baby time! The closer my due date got, the more anxious I was.

I was due in the middle of summer, and I was ready to get this baby out like most women in their last weeks of pregnancy. Peter had told me he had a gig offer out of the country, but he was not going to take it, because he would never wanna miss the birth of his child. But when he ended up taking it anyway, saying he was gonna be back in time, I couldn't believe it. I stayed calm and let him go. Why? Because I didn't want to have to tell my man what the right thing to do was; I wanted him to know what the right thing to do was. Obviously, he didn't. I was mad, but I honestly had a feeling that this baby was not going to come out before her due date. So, I didn't stress it. I also had been disappointed so many times, so I felt like, hell what is one more gonna do? In other words, I was used to it. Still, it was an unbelievable thing for him to do. I didn't trust Peter at this point, obviously, so him saying this was a money-making opportunity just went in one ear and out the other.

Thanks to today's technology, social media always let me know where Peter was, as fans would run into him and tweet or post pics of him. It was hard to do anything in public without being "exposed." So, when the day came and Peter had left, being that I was suspicious, I always opened those apps to get to the bottom of things. Sure enough, someone had seen Peter and his baby-mom at the airport and on the island he was headed. What I felt inside at this time—I'm surprised it didn't trigger me going into labor. . . . I was in distress!

When we spoke on the phone, I asked, "Is she there with you?" My voice was loud and agitated. "Don't lie!" I repeated the question a few times, becoming louder each time, and my heart was racing because, no matter what his answer was, I could feel that she was there. He had actually done this.

"No, she is not!" is what I got in response. This made me even more uneasy, because now I was not only feeling the pain from what was happening but also the pain of being lied to. Double the trouble for my heart! This was always the case when it came to lies being told to my face. Yes, I admit, a part of me sometimes just got confused and filled with uncertainty even to the point where I thought, *Am I crazy? What if he is telling the truth?* Those were the hardest moments. "Not knowing something hurts more than knowing something that hurts"—I wrote this in a song that I never finished. That was my thing about lies, and I still feel this way today.

I just had to learn that people have different ways of doing things. A man is not built like a woman, and not everyone loves like I do. And, yes, I, too, have told lies in my life, but—and I've had debates about this—I believe in different levels of lies. "A lie ain't a lie" to me.

A lie to cover up something you did, something so bad that it would crush someone's heart, is different from a lie told to cover up something that would only worry someone and isn't a "big deal." In the case of the latter, it is the actual lie that would be more disappointing than the act. Like a man who tells his woman that his phone was charging or he didn't hear it, when he really just wasn't in the mood to talk, compared to a man who says the same thing because he was fuckin' someone! That's a small lie versus a big one. It may take time, but I knew that big lies always got exposed and it was only a matter of time, so I told myself to chill until the time would come where I'd find out.

A few days later, at thirty-nine weeks pregnant, a week before my due date, my husband returned on Sunday evening July 27, 2014. We didn't fight. I had calmed my nerves by preparing the house for Cori's arrival. I was excited for him to see it. I didn't feel like arguing, and I didn't want any bad energy around me and in the house at this time (many times, this was the reason for me keeping quiet), so I just welcomed him with a hug and asked him if he had had a good trip. I also told him he was lucky the baby hadn't come yet. "I knew she wasn't coming; she's coming tonight," he replied as if he could predict it.

He seemed tired, but instead of passing out on the couch as he had so many other times, he said, "Go in the room and take your clothes off." Taken back, I paused for a moment, then looked at him, got up, and shook my head with half a smile. . . . Our sex life hadn't been consistent due to my pregnancy and had definitely been a little neglected. I had always been upset and Peter was always turned off because of that. So me being somebody that gets turned on by a man telling me what to do when it comes to sex, me, who hadn't been "getting it in" as much as I like to, me, who was nine months pregnant thinking about how long I was about to be sexless after birth, was just not going to turn down my husband whom I had been missing like crazy. I did just as he said.

About an hour later, I started feeling contractions. It was around 2 a.m. I just looked at Peter passed out as I cuddled up next to him trying to sleep through it, not really realizing that I was in labor. Peter kept waking up asking if I was okay, and around 5 a.m., I couldn't take it anymore; this pain was almost unbearable. We arrived at the hospital the morning of the 28th. I was in so much pain and completely shocked at finding out what it actually felt like. I had always thought I was less sensitive to physical pain than others, but this was hell.

I remember the hours passing and nothing happening, but I felt like I was dying. Shaking, freezing, sweating, even throwing up from the pain. It felt a hundred times worse than I had imagined. I had been begging the doctors for an epidural, but, for various reasons, they did not give it to me until twelve hours later.

My best friend and Peter were there with me, and I remember some other friends coming and going throughout the day and night I had my first baby. The cameras were also present, and I remember being annoyed because the hospital allowed only two people at a time in my room, and I was constantly asked who I wanted in the room. None of my family was there, and I was sad that my mom, my dad, or any of my sisters weren't able to be present. I thought of them a lot. I developed a fever during labor and had to get on more meds, which made me kind of drowsy, and a big portion of the time we spent in the hospital was a blur to me.

It was a long twenty-eight hours until my body was ready to push her out. But when it happened, man, I was glad I made it. She was beautiful. She was healthy and just so tiny. They laid her on me skin to skin, and I was instantly in love. I just looked at her big grey eyes and smelled her until the nurses took her from me to bring her to the NICU (neonatal intensive care unit) where she had to stay for three days because of all the meds I had gotten during labor.

The next 3 days were some of the hardest ever. I couldn't cope with not having my baby next to me. It did not feel right. I needed to be with my child. It made me cry. Even if I was able to spend as much time as I wanted in her room, in order to get some rest, I had to leave her behind, and I didn't wanna do that. I spent day and night sleeplessly sitting on a little chair next to her bed just looking at this human that I had created. I was shocked at never seeing other new moms hold or even just check on their babies who were in the same room as Cori. Like, how could they not wanna be next to their newborn? Didn't they feel with-drawal? It was incomprehensible to me.

Some of Peter's family came to see the newest addition, and I was always happy to see them. But I counted down the hours until I finally was able to take my baby home. I just wanted to be home with her. I didn't care about nothing else—I didn't care if Peter was or wasn't there, I didn't think about what was happening between him and I or all the problems we were having, and it didn't even matter to me that he was around the other woman while I was home with Cori. I just thought about my baby, that she was here and needed to be taken care of. I was in abso-lute mom mode. And I felt pure happiness when I looked at my child. Nothing mattered but beautiful Cori Pankey.

These feelings I had for my new love grew by the day, and in a blink of an eye, my life just wasn't about me anymore. It was about her. I didn't mind sacrificing for my baby. At all. As much work as it was, as much as it compli-cated things in my career, and as little as I would sleep, I loved it. And all of the things that I had worried about or wondered about becoming a mom came natural.

I loved seeing Peter with the baby. I loved how he wasn't new to this and knew exactly what he was doing in every situation. Seeing the love in his eyes when he held her was priceless. I knew he was a great father to all of the kids, but experiencing it with my own child made my love for him grow even more. And it was a sad thing because I knew I already loved him way too much.

Why, when I realized that I need to let go of him, was there always something that made my feelings for him stronger? Why was it that the more we headed for a breakup, the more we found ourselves inseparable? Love always trumped everything. I kept on keeping on saying to myself that I might just need more time, but then, one day, something clicked in me. I thought about every man I had loved. I thought about every situation and why it never worked out with anyone. I realized they all had left me. For whatever reason, they had ended it. Even if some of them weren't man enough to tell me it was over, I always noticed a change in them, and with that came an ending for us. I had never been the one. I had never broken up with someone I really loved (and I didn't even love them as much as my husband now). Was I not capable of such a thing? Maybe I wasn't. Maybe I needed to be broken up with to be able to let go of him. Because that is all I knew. Breaking my habit of waiting to be left to move on from a man was just something that I needed to work on, needed more time and help with.

If he wasn't leaving me, I wasn't leaving him.

"I wasn't strong enough."

"I don't have enough balls."

These are the things I would hear from people, and I can now say that they were right. But as much strength as it takes to leave someone you love, it also takes as much or more strength to stay with someone that hurts you. It's easy (for some people) to back out of something that's uncomfortable. And again, people are built differently. I felt weak for not leaving, but I felt strong for not giving up. . . .

The same year, Peter came to Germany and met my mom and dad for the first time (whom he loved and vice versa). Mom knew each and every thing that had happened between Peter and me, so she was always concerned, but Dad didn't have a clue. I never talked to him about it. He was still concerned, something he couldn't help with any man my sisters or I had ever been with, but that didn't take away from the fact that both of them saw the good person he is, perceived his kindness, and enjoyed his presence just as much as anyone else who ever spent time around him.

When that happened, it again all seemed like everything was coming together.

We were a family.

I have never shared the ideals for the perfect life that most women have. Find a man with money, get married at thirty, have children, buy a house, have a couple of cars, a dog in the backyard, and a couple of startup businesses to be able to say you're not just a housewife . . . basically a life where everything goes as planned.

All of that is nice, but I was just not that kind of girl. I never saw myself having that picture-perfect fairy tale life. Not that I wouldn't have liked that, but there were always other, more important things. "Perfect" has always been boring to me. That doesn't mean I didn't want a stable relationship with all the key qualities in a man. I was just always chasing after my own definitions of love, happiness, and freedom. I knew what they were, and I knew what I wanted. I needed to feel excitement. A real connection was the most important. Personality was what attracted me, never money or a great body. I did want a man that was mine! I wanted loyalty, honesty, and children with that person I loved, and I also wanted to make enough money to live comfortably. But never did I want to be dependent on someone, not even my significant other. I wanted the freedom to do me and whatever I wanted in life. Stand on my own feet. Create without rules and be the unique, one-of-a-kind artist I was born to become. And while I was doing good chasing a lot of these things, I felt that in love I was just not getting all I wanted, because I didn't wanna miss what I had in exchange for what I didn't.

I would have had to give up the connection, the excitement, the passion, the fun—the things that Peter and I had that mattered so much to me. There are no two people the same in this world, not even identical twins; I know this because I am one, so even if I did get those things with another, it would never have been the same.

CHAPTER 11:
What's Love Got to Do with It?

WHAT DO YOU DO when you know something's bad for you but you still can't let go?

Singer Christina Aguilera said that in one of her songs, and this wasn't the first time that I was relating to this question. That album of hers, *Stripped*, is one of my favorites because of how relatable it was to my circumstances. It was like she had been in my head while writing those songs.

Considering that I was now someone whose life was now regularly discussed by many top urban blogs as well as all over social media, I sometimes wondered why I allowed all of this to happen. But then again, it didn't bother me as much as it did before, and I already knew whatever they would say or try to make clear to me, and didn't care, because the fact was they just didn't have a clue. At this point, I was so numb to judgement.

For instance, people were stuck on the fact that Peter had gone on vacation with his "other" family while I, his wife, was about to give birth. In my opinion, yes, it was absolutely wrong, but they didn't acknowledge the fact that he, our new daughter, and I had gone on three vacations the following year. Furthermore, and he had been lying to her about it. People believed that what they saw on TV was the entire truth, but it was not, because the entire truth was not shown on TV. It doesn't make up for what he'd done to me, but all I'm saying is that people's views about us were, and always are, limited to the few minutes they witnessed unfold on the show. Simply put, it covered only a small portion of all the things that happened in our lives. It was bad, but it wasn't as bad as it seemed to those who watched with the limited information of an outsider. There was just so much more to the story, so much more conversation, and so many more critical things that happened. Things that we shared. A lot more love and laughter than people saw.

Also, I knew this was life, and this kind of thing was happening everywhere, all the time. Maybe this was not happening in the same form and fashion, but people getting cheated on, married men stepping out on their wives and even getting other women pregnant—these were not new concepts. Even people living double lives on a whole other level was not unheard of. I knew that this was bad because I was suffering so much, but it all seemed just so much worse because we were putting it on TV. Normal people don't broadcast this kind of stuff to the world.

Along with the negativity came sympathy. But in my case, that was something that happened over time. A little part of my soul came to shine through midst all the drama and short dialogues shown on TV, and I started getting more and more encouraging and comforting messages from fans. Women were now telling me that they were going through the same thing or something similar. Others disclosed that I'd helped them by putting my life out there. The thing that touched me the most was when ladies expressed how much my music touched them and made them see *me* underneath what TV alone had portrayed, beyond the face and the side of me that was shown on TV. "When I listen to your music, I see who you are"—I loved hearing that from people. It felt good that the real me was perceived through my way of expression. It felt good to know that I did have people in my corner.

By the time my daughter turned one, the other woman and I had started talking to each other cordially. We would even talk on the phone sometimes, mostly about kids, and I was sincere in wanting to build a relationship as it was fact that we all were a family now. Time had made the animosity die down, not completely, but speaking for myself, I was looking at her more and more the same way I was looking at myself. We were one, we were women, we had something in common, we were dealing with the same thing, the same man, the same lies, the same disappointments—it was relatable talking to her, and I tried putting myself into her shoes and imagining how all that had happened was affecting her. Even if it was different, and possibly even harder, than it was for me. I realized that if I were her, I would probably be doing the same thing she was. I wouldn't stop sleeping with the man I had been with for thirteen years, the man I love. I wouldn't be able to let go and move on just like that. But one thing I would have done differently is that I would be real about it and not pretend to be done with him for public affirmation.

However, it meant something to me that things were changing. I even had visions of us giving each other a heartfelt hug and breaking down together. I was having breakdowns all the time in the presence of no one but my own self, thinking she must feel the pain too, even if she didn't show it in the same way I did. Anyway, I was envisioning a real hug, not one of those fake ones that are so common, especially here in America. Whenever I did something like that in my life, it was real and from the heart; I never had vicious motives or strategies and plans to get something beneficial to me.

Thinking that she was as genuine as I was may have been dumb, but hey, I cannot help but see the good in people. Beyond our differences, she was a loving mother and woman. However, I had a reputation of being naïve. In my mind, I wasn't; I was overly skeptical and questioned everything! I started getting confused as to how much I could trust her, especially when Peter would tell me how much she despised me. It made sense that she did, but he was also untrustworthy, so again I wasn't sure who to believe, the person who I knew loves me but lies all the time or someone who pretty much hates me and is a very calculated individual. It sometimes felt like a conspiracy. But as much as she was publicly proclaiming that Peter and her were through and "just friends," and as nice as she had become towards me, I really felt as if she was accepting me and Peter's relationship. Not necessarily respecting, but accepting. Leaving us be. I knew that Peter was still uncomfortable showing any kind of affection to me in her presence, so being the considerate person I am, I would just play along and, out of respect for the jabs her heart had taken, not "be his wife" for a few hours. It was definitely weird whenever all three of us were in the same room. I would just always imagine how things would be between them when I was not around, knowing how different things were between us when she wasn't around.

With that said, my gut was always telling me that I needed to expect the worst, despite the fact that we were 'friendly' with each other now. They had both been lying when it came down to it. In interviews, they were asked whether or not they still have sex? The answer from both of them was always "No, we are strictly co-parenting." I'll admit, I didn't believe it. I had always hoped that I was wrong. In the back of my mind, I knew they were far from over. It became even clearer, when Peter became disinterested in sex with me. There was a phase that lasted a few months. He would blame it on our constant fights or a few times on simply 'being tired'. I immediately knew he was getting it somewhere else; especially since he was the one who had taught me that 'if a man doesn't wanna have sex with you, he is having it with someone else'...we had talked about it many times. He would tell me that before I even came into the picture, his woman must have known he was stepping out on her because she recognized that they weren't sleeping together for months at a time. Now, it was me in this very position and everyday felt like a nightmare because I was being cheated on again. I was not satisfied at home either, in our bed! I would sometimes think, if I can't take myself out of this position, I gotta find something that can, or at the very least something that can make me feel better and less like a fool. I thought that maybe if I decided to do something behind his back, it would change things, and make him want me again. I even thought that maybe me finding comfort elsewhere would make him leave me, which would not be a bad thing.

Right around this time, I was approached by an NBA player whom I'm not going to name. It was on one of those few nights I got to go out, now that I had a baby at home. Every time I did get to go out, I wanted to be out with my husband but things were bad between us and it seemed that he was always doing his own thing. He would often say "I'll meet you there" and then never show up nor come home at all… this happened many times. But I always tried. On this night, I was at a viewing party with my girl and I texted Peter "come, there's a bunch of NBA players sweatin me" in hopes of making him jealous. I didn't care about them, I really just wanted my husband, but truth was, he didn't want me as much. His actions were proof. I was feeling like I was going to get stood up again, so I started drinking and forcing myself to have fun alone. When I got asked for my number, I didn't hesitate in giving it to this guy. He was hot to me. The most famous one at the table, I'd say. I kept thinking that this was all so ironic. So I started talking to him. I put his name in my phone as "Ro" because we met at the spot named The Royal. I tried to do the thing that Peter does. Lie. It didn't sit well with me, nor did I feel good while doing it. I also learned that Ro was married. My girl told me that night… Was that my problem? No. But, I did consider that this was out of line and something I should have learned not to do by now. However, the situation I was in, made me feel selfish. What can I say? I wasn't the only one being selfish here. I was putting myself in a position to be his other woman, or should I say 'one of' his other women, because we all know what most NBA players' lifestyles are like.

Anyway, the night this whole thing started, at The Royal, Peter unexpectedly popped up right after I had given out my number to the guy. I felt happy and guilty at the same time. I felt like Peter deserved to get cheated on, but I also felt like this wasn't me and I would never do this if it were not for what he was putting me through. I felt that it was also not right because he had a wife...so I slowed my roll, didn't talk to him unless he hit me up.. I never ended up cheating because of that.. Or was it because I got caught? Who knows? All I know is that I'm glad that I did, because it was wrong of me to start anything with Ro to begin with. Being a player was just not me nor was it something I could master. I failed miserably as Peter found all of my text messages in my iPad one night. It included messages between me and my girl talking about just what I was trying to do, cheat.

Although I hadn't actually cheated as in having sex, I know Peter was hurt. Even if he didn't show it one bit. He just became really cold and kept saying how much it makes him look at me different.

Now, I was considered "the bad guy". This whole thing had just made everything worse.. And it made Peter do something else, which I learned 5 months later...

In August of 2015, Peter, our baby girl, and I took a trip to Jamaica. It was one of those "make up" trips as obviously we were still and again having bigtime issues that seemed never ending. But I always looked forward to going away with him because I knew he would be with me and only me. There was no "not coming home" or him disappearing. We were together the entire time on our vacay. Every time Peter said, "Let's go away," I didn't hesitate to say yes, because of how much he was not diverted when in another place. I just loved it. Time with him was worth putting the issues to the side. Always.

I was looking forward to this getaway; however, something was off.

My baby had just turned one, and I had just started feeling it again, the feeling I knew as a sign for change in my body. My love and desire for coffee in the morning had gone, just smelling it made me wanna throw up. And when I thought about sipping cocktails by the beach in Jamaica, I was disgusted. It had happened. I was pregnant again. I knew before we left for our vacay, and even Peter had noticed. But I didn't take a test until we arrived at our resort.

It was clear to me that the test was going to be positive once I took it. I was unsure how to feel. One side of me felt that this was meant to happen; the other just said, "Fuck!" Although I still loved Peter to death, I knew what kind of messed up marriage I was in. Did I really wanna keep on expanding and building on something I knew wasn't making me entirely happy? The same questions came up that I'd had almost two years before. But I'd envisioned myself with two children, not one, and I had always been saying and feeling that I wanted more. Again, I was on a beautiful island, this time with the man I loved, feeling like shit. This really wasn't my thing. . . . Other than feeling low physically, we had a good time until the last day. I got a text from the other woman asking me if I was with Peter. We kept going back and forth about how I thought she would have known we were away, and then she told me that Peter had once again lied and said he was on a business trip.

"Why lie to her when y'all are not together?" I'd ask Peter this *all* the time, and he would answer, "I don't wanna be bothered with shit; she would ruin our vacay." Basically, he'd tell me about how she would start arguing with him, how she was still hurt, how she wouldn't let him enjoy his vacation with me. It was absolutely crazy that things were still like this after more than two years.

However, I was talking to her now, and by doing so, it became clear to me that it was a reality. They were actually still together. What was going on between them wasn't just "co-parenting" or "being friends" or "getting along for the kids"—he was still as much in a relationship with her as he was with me. Only, I was open about it, which made me the stupid one. They were being on the low. And with that being the case, Peter wasn't doing anything to her; at least, it looked that way. Maybe they didn't say it out loud or even to each other, but the way their relationship was still functioning was not something you could label "separated." The only separation that had happened was spatial. And even that wasn't actually the case because Peter would come and go to her house whenever he wanted and kick up his feet on the couch as if it was his home. The communication was as constant as it was between two people who were a couple. And maybe they didn't hold hands in public or sleep together as much as before, but they were always around each other, even if "for the kids." It just always felt like my husband had another woman, and he absolutely did. So in this moment, even though it was obvious before, it was clearer now that sex wasn't something that had stopped either. Ever.

Coming back from Jamaica, I was turned off from everything, and I was hurt as ever like so many times before. Still filming the TV show, it all came to blows a couple of weeks later as I popped up at her house to confront them both. It seemed that, when cameras were rolling, he was always a bit more cautious of his ways and words, trying to make up for what he had done to her. It almost felt like he was acting. My feelings seemed to always come second when it came to TV world, because even though he knew he had put me through a lot as well, in his mind, it didn't compare with the amount of embarrassment he put her through by publicly exposing a marriage that she was completely unaware of. At the same time, it could have been that he was more real and honest when the other woman was present, and what I would experience in these moments was the actual truth of things. I believe it was the latter.

I knew I was going to hear that same old "he's still sleeping with me, he's still doing this and that, blah, blah"; however, I knew he was doing and saying a lot of things out of guilt.

What people got to see was him apologizing to her and playing me, him trying to get back with her and cheating on me, him waking up at her house and not coming home to me. This was the subject of our story, this was the dilemma I was in on screen, but this was not my reality. Because, even though that was accurate, he was doing the same things in reverse. Still, on this day, I once again got shaken heavily by his words, and I felt that if he could say these things on camera he might as well mean them. And maybe he did.

All in all, I was aware of the fact that Peter probably wouldn't have married me if he had thought it through, if he hadn't acted and lived in the moment. But everything that had followed our precipitous decision had let me feel that with a couple of exceptions he had no regrets. However, he later explained and corrected his statement. Hearing that he sometimes felt I was a "mistake" and "something that went too far" came unexpected and hurt like hell.

Maybe my emotional state was extra fragile because I was pregnant again, I am not sure, but I just lost all sense of control over my actions. This ended up being one of our biggest scenes, as I hit him in the face and ran out yelling that I was pregnant. Peter had wanted me to keep quiet about it, but in this moment, what Peter wanted did not matter to me one bit. What the cameras didn't catch was Peter packing his things and leaving in rage following the incident, not saying a word to me. We didn't speak or see each other for the next week or so.

It was mid-September 2015, and he left town for a few days to go see his daughters in New Orleans after the big fight. I wanted out. I wanted to be strong enough to say, "Fuck this," and finally leave. Breakup without making up. This had been going on for too long, but I knew that my being pregnant kept me tied to him, kept me vulnerable, kept me hopeful and forgiving. It started crossing my mind that if I "got rid of this," the pain would never let me make things right again, and I could never be with him after that, which I thought was exactly what I needed. However, I got extremely sick every time my mind started considering abortion. I would wake up one day and think, *I am going to have this baby no matter what.* Then, I'd wake up the next day and feel that I needed to terminate the pregnancy and, with that, the relationship with Peter for good.

Days went by, and every day I felt life growing inside of me made it harder to decide what I was going to do. The amount I cried during this time was insane; it had my head hurting twenty-four hours a day. I couldn't even think straight. I was broken. I was torn. I was lost. I even talked to my mom, and she, as always, told me she would support whatever decision I made. I was desperate for help. But no one could help me. It was my body that this was happening to, and no one but me was able to live with the consequences following this decision.

After already announcing the news on camera, I felt that I needed to just have this baby because what would I tell the producers? What would the people who watch us on the show think? Everyone would think I lied, and that was something I did not want to happen. Then, I thought I could in fact just lie and say I had a miscarriage. Or say, "I lied—I was just mad!" However, thinking about it, I didn't want that either. I just wanted to keep it real unlike so many other women who have gone through the same thing publically. I could name a few, but I won't go there. That meant, if I was going to terminate this pregnancy, I would have to own up to it and say that I did. Just to explain why I was not pregnant anymore. I swear, my mind was spinning!

A whole week went by, and I didn't hear from Peter. When he finally did texted me, he said nothing but hurtful words, which pushed me even more towards the decision I didn't want to make. He was clearly still mad about me hitting him in the face and for not keeping my mouth shut about the pregnancy. I knew he didn't want another child. But in my mind, he didn't have the right to feel any kind of way about me being pregnant, because, truth is, I wasn't pregnant alone. *We* were pregnant. He had made me pregnant by doing what the both of us had wanted to do and what we had always done. Make love.

Yet, he was mad. He must have not been thinking when he wrote, "I hope you're not really pregnant," at the end of our exchange. I believe it was the following day that I woke up in tears (once again), drained by the thoughts which consumed my nights. Jazz had been in town and knew of my dilemma. She knew how hurt I was, but she was not expecting to hear me say this morning, "I'm doing it."

Although she just said, "Okay," I saw the sadness on her face. I had made a trip to the abortion clinic a few days before, but had left with a disgusting taste in my mouth thinking and feeling that it was just not right. However, here I was, back at the clinic ready to pay for them to end everything. Thinking back, I really felt as if I was doing it to free myself from this relationship. I was exactly nine weeks pregnant, and I knew this was the last day I had the option to take a pill as opposed to getting it done surgically. I had made my decision, but when the nurse brought me the papers to sign and came into the room with the tablet that was going to kill my fetus, I broke down right in front of her.

She could feel my pain. "You don't really wanna do this, do you?"

"No," I said.

"Go outside," she responded, "sit in your car, make some phone calls—do whatever you need to do—and when you're ready, you can come back. If you change your mind, don't come back."

I was such a mess I just nodded my head and walked outside.

I thought about calling Peter, but I didn't. He hadn't been here, and I knew running to the person who was at the center of all this was not the right move. So, I called Jazz. She just said I needed to follow my heart. She told me to call Mom, but Mom didn't answer. I sat in my car for an hour, once again thinking about how having this baby would make everything harder and more complicated, but how having this abortion would just be the easy way out . . . not realizing that it was going to break my heart even more than it already was broken.

So, I went back inside and quickly swallowed the pill. It was over. I knew there was no more turning back; I had just done what no one, including myself, had seen coming.

The following night was without a doubt one of the roughest nights of my life. I kept waking up in pools of blood. It felt like I was just having a bad nightmare. Every hour, I ran to the bathroom, crying harder and harder as I saw my body discharge all that was growing inside of me. Every hour, it hurt more, and every hour, I got weaker. My bed was covered in blood, and I ended up staying in the bathroom because I wouldn't stop bleeding.

At some point, I passed out from exhaustion. The next morning, still lying on the bathroom floor, I yelled my sister's name until she came to help me get up. She was shocked at the sight—it looked like a massacre had happened. I will never forget how happy I was that it was over and, at the same time, how much it hurt.

Before I forced myself to clean up, I took pictures of the astonishing mess and sent them to Peter with the caption, "I'm not pregnant anymore. Hope you're happy now."

Unlike other times, he responded within seconds. "I didn't want you to do that," he said. "My heart just dropped." He apologized for all that he had done to hurt me. But I just wondered why it took me doing this to make him feel sorry. It was too late. . . .

Regardless of how wrong he had acted, I could feel his sadness. He just really hadn't thought I would ever go and have an abortion. But it was what it was now, and all I tried to focus on was getting over it, getting past this, and moving on from it. Not beat myself up. It wasn't easy.

Peter spent entire month of October trying to make up for our loss as if it was all his fault, and he knew that he was part of my pain, but ultimately, I had made the decision to end the pregnancy. So, even though I did not blame him entirely, it was hard for me to even look at him at times. However, seeing his effort also made it hard for me to go through with my plan to not talk to him anymore. Day by day, I would think, *If I stay with him, I might as well have kept the baby.* But the Peter that was here now was a new Peter. He was all the things I never had in him but had always waited for. Didn't this seem familiar. . . .

I found myself still right inside the never-ending circle. Yes, it had been weeks since the abortion, but I was still regretful and extremely hurt. I needed support and comfort. Again, Peter was the only one there to give me just that, he was the only one who was able to reduce the pain. No one else could, no matter how hard they tried.

Needless to say, my plan hadn't worked. I just never thought I would ever get this Peter that I now had, a Peter who was all about me, who called me when he was late, who let me know where he was at all times, who came home to me every single night, who prioritized me and my feelings, who was just trying his very best to finally give me what I deserved, who out of the blue said, "Let's go away; pick a place, and let's get away from the bullshit." I just did not know how to resist. I needed a getaway after this traumatic experience.

My baby Cori, Peter, and I took a quick trip to Miami a couple weeks later in the beginning of November. Though I was far from over it, on a scale from one to ten (ten being best!), things between Peter and me went to a ten! I knew he felt bad about the whole abortion thing, so much so that he would even say things like, "I owe you another baby," and, "We're gonna make another one." It would just break my heart because I knew it was wrong for me to even like hearing that after having just killed a baby. But it almost seemed as if there was something else he was trying to make up for. He was just so incredibly loving, and even making love felt different—just so much more intense. I couldn't help but think that something was about to happen. This was just too good to be true. A woman's intuition is always right, as I learned soon after. . . .

Anyway, this little vacation we were on was amazing. He even posted pictures of us on social media, which he never did, to let me know that this time there weren't any lies being told. We spent the days at the beach, walking up and down the strip, and the nights making love . . . so much love. It was consoling.

Then on November 6th, it happened. Peter had been telling me for a few days that he had something to tell me, and I just knew it was going to be bad. I gave him his time and didn't bother to ask, but I will never forget the way my heart dropped down to the floor and I couldn't feel my legs when he finally dropped the bomb. He started talking about the other woman. . . .

I just kept asking, "What? What now? You're still sleeping with her!?"

He hesitated before finally answering, "She says she might be pregnant."

As I've said before, it felt like I just got stabbed in my heart, and I actually asked him why he didn't just take a knife and stab me, because that would have hurt less. I had never felt that kind of pain ever before in my life. There are no words to describe the exact way I felt. It was just too much. I broke down for the hundredth time. Did I not just have to pick myself up from being so low? I asked Peter to tell me everything, but he just said, "I don't know. All I know is she is very far along."

She was further along than I would have been had I not aborted my baby. In fact, she had been pregnant since summer, and it was November! Why did I have to feel this? I talked to myself in a loud voice the entire time as I walked away from him—people must have thought I was a crazy person—saying, "Why, why, why? I can't take this." I disappeared for a while, and I can just remember my phone going off with texts from him saying he was sorry, wishing I was still pregnant, and listing all the things that he wanted to do to make it better. But there was nothing. Nothing he could do to make it better. Nothing at all.

After every painful event, it seemed there was another even more painful one just waiting to occur. It didn't feel fair to me when people would blame me for what I was going through, saying I put myself here and was now getting what I deserved. Yes, I had stayed in this relationship through more than enough disappointments, but I had decided over and over again that I wasn't going to allow this to keep happening—I just didn't succeed. . . . Did that make me stupid? If anything, it showed I was not strong enough yet! But what do you do when you don't succeed at something? You try again, and with every try, I gained strength.

However, in this moment, I just felt defeated, as if I had been fighting so hard for so long and, in the end, got knocked out. I knew I was going to have to back away, and I knew that was exactly what the other woman had always wanted and she was going to get it. There was no more fight in me. I told Peter to tell her congratulations and wished them well.

Even though I still stuck around a little while longer, from the moment I found out there was a baby coming and it wasn't mine, after just having dealt with the painful experience of abortion, I stopped fighting and just let things happen.

Today, I know that the love we made in Miami had more meaning than anything. We conceived our second daughter that week, five weeks after having an abortion and right before learning the news. I got accused of "spitefully getting pregnant again." People thought I wanted to have a second baby now only because the other woman was pregnant, but the truth is that I was already pregnant when I found out. Yes, I thought it was unfair that she got to have the baby that I wanted, but having a child to get back at someone was not in my nature. Actually, I think that it is a reflection on whoever would say so instead.

People wondered why I decided to keep the baby this time around and my answer is simple: I was not going to have two abortions within three months. One was bad enough, and it's something that still hurts to think about. I just wasn't going to make the same mistake twice. Some may say the mistake was getting pregnant again, but I don't think so. In love, things happen. And if you love like me, you sometimes lose control.

CHAPTER 12:
P.S. I Love You

ON AUGUST 9TH, 2016, I gave birth to a beautiful baby girl. With my heart, I affectionately named her Bronx.

Today, I am the proud mother of two little girls that make my heart sing the most beautiful melodies. The tattoo on my right arm says "my first love is a melody." Today, these girls are my melody. They have brought back my desire to sing. And yes, I do sing to them and with them daily. They keep me going. They simply give me happiness and are the main reason I smile every day of my life. They do drive me crazy but I honestly don't know where I would be without them.

Going through everything that happened over the past 4 years, including losing my creativity and dealing with writer's block, while at other times prosperously blooming (see my music releases "I Am Part 1" and "I Am Part 2" and my first full album "My Music" which I am all very proud of), I realized that this is the life of a real artist. I am a real artist. You cannot force anything. You have to let it come to you. That's how you know it's real. In art and in love.

I now realize that it (love & art) will always find me. Even when it felt like I had lost it all, I now know that I had only gained new perspective. Recently, I sat down at my piano in my fairly new apartment in North Hollywood and began to play. After so many failed attempts, I found myself singing a new song "Back to What I Know".

"...So tonight I'm gonna listen to this song I have inside, find the words that I've been trying to find, let go of what it was that had me feeling blind, go back to what I know is mine."

Leaving New York was a rapid decision that I made without a plan. It was an instinctual move that happened out of desperation for change. When my daughter Cori began to wipe away my tears, I knew, I had to get out of the space I was in. When I looked at my piano and realized my fingers hadn't touched it in weeks, I felt that I needed to do something different. Every time I tried, I failed, so moving away was just another 'try' to make myself better.

It was my attempt to change something, instead of waiting for change to happen.

Getting back to caring about me was the goal. Did it work? To a certain degree, it did. I cry a lot less and I am healing. I spent the majority of my pregnancy alone (by choice). Alone with my daughter Cori, because she was who helped me get up with a smile every morning, and simply to keep going.. Reflecting, relaxing and just breathing was my main focus. I'll admit, I had a hard time adjusting to a life without the man I loved and without the father of my girls. I even had many sleepless nights filled with doubt about this being the right move. Leaving Peter alone, was the hardest thing I have ever done.

As I write this, we have been living separated for the past 7 months and our relationship still has its ups and downs. The difference is that he doesn't consume me and my emotions and thoughts. I don't worry about where he is at night. I think about where I wanna be in a few years instead. I have gotten used to the fact that he is living his life (whatever that means). It still hurts but I have found new ways to survive it. We do love each other, and I will not lie and say I'm over him, I'm still in love with my favorite person. He still makes me smile and sometimes makes me sad but I have taken one step at a time towards reaching new goals, one after another. When I left, I promised myself to work on accepting the fact that he is not capable of giving me what I need now. And I have, with the help of therapy, accepted that I cannot have him in the way I wanted. I've also made up my mind about what I will and will not accept, which reminds me of my latest song "More Than You", which I have written while writing this book.

"Loving me is a privilege and loving me is a win, loving me should be appreciated, my heart not broken, I'm worth more than an option and no doubt I'm more than 2, I'm the one who leaves this knowing I deserve more than you"

I don't think this whole experience has changed the way I love. Nothing, could ever change the way I love, but I do believe it's made it harder for any man that might come into my life from this point on.

I'd like to think that I have learned from my mistakes, so that one day when I am open again to love, I will know what to do different. I will know what I am getting myself into, and if I don't, then I will not get myself into it. Lesson one! And there are so many more...

I am, after all, a very forgiving person. Theologian Reinhold Niebuhr said it best "forgiveness is the final form of love." I love that quote. I live by it. When I posted that quote recently, it got misunderstood by many who thought I meant forgiving equals accepting or allowing. The point that I was trying to make for myself was that I'm not mad. It's not in my character to stay mad even at someone who has really wronged me. I would often tell my husband, "I'm not mad, I'm just sad." This still applies to us. However, I am slowly but surely moving away from being sad. Luckily for me, you can only stay sad for so long, as time heals all wounds.

I still think back often to my days growing up and how having sisters was always such a privilege, so seeing my girls bonding so early on is amazing. When Bronx cries, my 2 year old Cori is the first one to be concerned. It's beautiful.

One day my children will be old enough to read this and they will learn the truth about everything and how they came to be in this world. What's most important in this, is that they will know, they are here because their dad and their mom loved each other. They will know how much we both love them and I am hopeful towards the thought of them being close with all of their siblings, even the ones that have another woman as their mother.

As far as the other woman that I spoke of most frequently in this book, we are good! I guess I can say that we have learned to respect one another as mothers and women who love hard. We know that neither of us will ever stop being family to the man who created ours. I am only looking to make things better from this point on. We have a long way to go but how horrible is it to live with hate or animosity inside of you towards anyone? I've never had 'beef' with someone in my life before all of this occurred and I never ever want to again. Having peace is very valuable to me these days.

My girls and their happiness comes first, even before mine. Yes, it is also important for them to have their father around but I had to make a choice. Trying to regain my peace was the top priority. For them! When they see me happy, they are happy. When I'm happy, I want to make them happier. And when they smile, I know that I have succeeded.

I have never been someone to give up on anything but before I became a mom, I was much more nonchalant about getting things done. Now that I have my girls, things have to get done whether it's little things or big things, I just do it! And I'm sure a lot of moms can relate. Whatever I need can wait. And people ask me all the time "how do you do it with two little ones by yourself and no family around?" i just answer with "I don't know, I just do it." I know that I am not the only one.

These days, I take one day at a time, focusing on motherhood and getting back to my calling. I've got music on my mind. It's been a big part, if not the biggest of my journey as told in this book. Music is also the root of my reason for being where I am. Coming to America, meeting Peter and having these amazing babies.. Without music, none of this would have happened. I also know that music will help me move forward. There were times that I was too damaged to do what I do best, to write a song or even just play my instruments, is in the past. I am more than ready to do it again and somehow, I feel my best is yet to come, musically.

Along with this story, I am releasing a new EP entitled "Music in My Room" consisting of 5 acoustic songs that I wrote and composed on the piano over the years. These songs happened throughout the course of this very journey and every single one was mentioned in this book. I still dream big and I believe in the saying "everything gets better with age".

So here I am writing the last chapter of my first book. It started out as something that I did for myself, but now that I'm sharing my story, I am thrilled and proud to have made it to this place in my life.

And as I'm writing these last words, sitting in a cafe, enjoying the California sunshine, holding my 2 month old while she is sleep and browsing through pictures to edit for my ep cover, I'm thinking back to how powerful I felt those days in Brooklyn when I had nothing but my gift and love for myself. I am also reminded of how powerful I am now, being alone yet feeling stronger than ever. I reflect upon how I still do it all and can do it all and how much more life I have to live, and how thankful I am that I am able to live it the way I want to, simply because I fearlessly decided to just go for it.

ACKNOWLEDGMENTS

I want to thank my two daughters Cori and Bronx for giving me strength to continue pursuing my career and my dream and for giving me inspiration when I had none. Lastly, for motivating me to tell my story as I did with this book.

With that said I also want to thank their dad, Peter, because if not for him and all I went through because of him, I wouldn't have my daughters who bring me happiness everyday, and I wouldn't have this very story to tell.

I want to acknowledge my sisters Sophie and Jazz as well as my parents who all contributed to this story and my journey in massive ways. I want to thank Esther and Nycole for the part they have played in my life as friends and for the continuous support. I am also thankful for all of my exes, the ones I don't speak to anymore and the guys I just dated, for making me learn the lessons I needed to learn in order to know what I don't want in a partner.

My publishing company 13th & Joan, especially Ardre Orie for making the process of becoming an author so easy and always encouraging to write from the heart, and helping and advising me when I was stuck. Lastly, I want to say I love my fans. I don't say it enough but I'm so thankful for you. Thank you for taking the time to read my work, for paying attention and for motivating me to continue striving towards my calling.

—AB

ABOUT THE AUTHOR

AMINA BUDDAFLY who was born and raised in Hamburg, Germany started out with a singing group consisting of her and her two sisters. Amina and the group signed their first record deal at the age of 15. The group moved to New York in 2002 and has released music on labels such as Island Def Jam and J Records under the name "Black Buddafly" for the past 12 years. Amina, the former lead singer of the group, went indie and solo in 2010 and has now grown an enormous following being on VH1's hit TV show "Love and Hip Hop". Today, Amina is an artist, author, mother and entrepreneur blazing new trails for her career.

LOOK FOR AMINA'S NEW ALBUM

Music in my room
Amina Buddafly

CONNECT WITH AMINA

WEBSITE: WWW.IAMAMINA.COM

IG: @AMINABUDDAFLY

FACEBOOK: WWW.FACEBOOK.COM/IAMAMINA

TWITTER: @AMINABUDDAFLY

SNAP: @ABUDDAFLY1

CPSIA information can be obtained
at www.ICGtesting.com
Printed in the USA
LVOW01s0143290317
528829LV00006B/8/P